D0965447

A FORGIVING GOD IN AN UNFORGIVING WORLD

Ron Lee Davis
with
James D. Denney

HARVEST HOUSE PUBLISHERS
Eugene, Oregon 97402

The names of certain persons and places have been changed in order to protect the privacy of the individuals involved.

Except where otherwise indicated, all Scripture quotations in this book are taken from the Holy Bible, New International Version, Copyright © 1978 by the New York International Bible Society. Used by permission.

A FORGIVING GOD IN AN UNFORGIVING WORLD

Copyright © 1984 by Ron Lee Davis
Published by Harvest House Publishers
Eugene, Oregon 97402

Library of Congress Catalog Card Number 84-081215
ISBN 0-89081-431-7 (trade edition)
ISBN 0-89081-469-4 (cloth edition)

All rights reserved. No portion of this book may be reproduced in any form without the written permission of the Publisher.

Printed in the United States of America.

Dedicated to my family:
Shirley, Rachael, and Nathan;

to our families of faith
in the Midwest, and now in California;

and to all the agents of
unconditional love, acceptance, and forgiveness
who have come into my life
and who have truly written these pages
as they have reflected the
grace of God to me.

Acknowledgments

The greatest model of unconditional love, acceptance, and forgiveness in my life was my father. Throughout my childhood I had the rich privilege of watching Dad express his forgiveness to our family and to others in his family of faith, the small-town church in Iowa where he served as pastor for nearly 25 years. Having given my life to Christ and grown up in a home where forgiveness was regularly experienced, I feel deeply grateful.

Despite the rich, nurturing experience of so much forgiving love in my early life, I have to admit a strong sense of my own inadequacy to the task of writing a book about forgiveness. Throughout my life, and even throughout the time I've been writing these pages, I have experienced many times of feeling unforgiven by God or other people, of feeling incapable of forgiving myself, and of striving to achieve forgiveness and reconciliation with Christian friends with whom I have had some tough, honest struggles.

I still wrestle with forgiveness in all its dimensions. I'm still in the process—a lifelong process of discovering what it means to know the unconditional love, acceptance, and forgiveness of God, and to express those qualities to other people.

I am grateful to my father and mother, who first began to teach me by their lives about forgiveness. I would also like to express my appreciation to others who have played a part in the development of this book.

My dear and special friend, Jim Denney, has contributed to the shaping of this book what I alone could never have hoped to achieve. I am deeply grateful that God in His timing and by His grace has brought Jim into my life, not only because of his rich insights and wise observations in regard to the themes of this book, but because of his loving spirit and his friendship.

Much of the material in this book has been presented to my family of faith at First Presbyterian Church in Fresno, California, and I am grateful for them and for so many in our fellowship who have been like a prism, reflecting the many colors of God's grace, love, and forgiveness to me.

Tess Mott, Debbie Denney, Kent Garborg, Stan Jantz, Tim Rolen, Gene McCarty, Linda Osborne, Meredith Hicks, Steven and Gayle Jaurena, Jim and Carol Gartung, Russ and Jan Koch, Hilary Chittick, and Janet McClenahan have all played a significant part in the development of this book, and I am thankful for them and for their friendship in my life.

I must express my appreciation to Bob Hawkins, president of Harvest House Publishers. It was only through Bob's encouragement and belief in me as a Christian communicator and author that I was able to write this book. To Bob, Eileen Mason, and the rest of the team at Harvest House, my deepest thanks.

Special appreciation must go to my wife, Shirley, who carefully critiqued each chapter, and whose suggestions and encouragement have been so important to the creation of this book.

There have been scores of friends whom God has brought into my life, and who have helped me to discover the freedom and joy that can be found in knowing that we are unconditionally loved, accepted, and forgiven. In this freedom comes the opportunity to love, accept, and forgive others in ways that bring healing and renewal within the Christian family today. For the multitude of believers in Christ who have invested in my life I will always be grateful.

—Ron Lee Davis

Contents

Foreword

Sometimes it is embarrassing to have an old friend ask you to write a foreword for his newest book. There is such an avalanche of new books for the Christian community that one tends to wonder if we need one more. This is not the case with *A Forgiving God in an Unforgiving World*. My friend, Ron Lee Davis, has written a book that should unlock the door to the availability of God's love and power to many. It is both simple and profound and is full of life-changing truth.

Relevance should be the first criterion for any Christian book. The gospel is quintessentially relevant. Jesus said, "I came that they might have life, and have it more abundantly." Religion is often esoteric, and theology is sometimes dull, but God Himself is never dull. He always meets us at the growing edge of our lives.

This book is about forgiveness. There is no single issue more important for our personal or corporate survival today than this matter of forgiveness. It is crucial to our international survival. It is crucial to the survival of every institution and structure. But in this book Ron Lee Davis deals primarily with the personal dimensions of forgiveness and that is the very heart of the human problem.

Can I forgive my enemy? Can I forgive those people who are either consciously trying to harm me or who are, by their very indifference, obstacles to my growth and fulfillment? Then there is the question of forgiving my friend. Can I forgive those people who harm me inadvertently, sometimes with perfectly good intentions? Some of us had parents who deliberately intended to harm us emotionally or even physically. But probably more of us had parents who loved us deeply and yet their mistakes have caused us lasting harm and great pain. Can I forgive myself when I have been my own worst enemy? For most of us, this happens with embarrassing frequency. And then there is the great question of whether or not I can forgive God for what He has or has not done in my life or in the lives of those I love. This book deals with these intensely personal questions.

For me, another criterion for a "must read" Christian book is whether or not it is biblical. There is so much advice being disseminated today by Christians to Christians which may be interesting and even helpful but not biblical. Ron Lee Davis has his feet rooted in Scripture, and he is thoroughly biblical in his approach to this vital subject of forgiveness.

A further criterion for any Christian book centers on whether or not the author speaks from personal experience, bringing existential wisdom and light from a biblical basis to everyday problems and situations. I have known Ron long enough to know that he is in Henri Nouwen's words a "wounded healer." His own experiences give him a firsthand understanding of the cost and power of forgiveness.

Finally, any good and helpful Christian book is concerned with application. The author ought to give us a strategy for applying God's powerful truth to the personal pain and hurt of our lives and the lives of those around us. We need handles by which we can lay hold on the power of God. Ron Lee Davis gives us those handles without giving us blueprints. *A Forgiving God in an Unforgiving World* is a liberating book that will release many by the power of God's Spirit and by the grace of His gospel.

—*Bruce Larson*
University Presbyterian Church
Seattle, Washington

1

God Forgives

When I was 18 and growing up in a small town in Iowa, one of my best friends was a young man named Jim Harlan. We were freshmen in college together, classmates, and fellow members of the school basketball team and the student council.

My friend Jim had a dream—a dream of gleaming chrome and steel and coal-black rubber that stood in the display window of the motorcycle dealership at the edge of town. One day, after months of saving his earnings from a part-time job, Jim fulfilled that dream. He walked into that cycle shop, plunked his cash on the counter, and roared off the lot astride his cherished Honda machine.

During the next few days the rumble of Jim Harlan's engine and the fragrance of his exhaust fumes graced our little town during every moment of his spare time. He polished his cycle until it glinted in the moonlight. He gave rides to anyone brave enough to straddle the backseat.

After he had owned that motorcycle for about a week, he was riding east on Main Street in the late afternoon, as the sun was hanging at eye-level in the west. Rolling up to Main from a side street, driving a large sedan, was Mr. Smith. As Jim approached the intersection out of the glare of the sun, Mr. Smith paused at the stop sign, squinted into the sun—then proceeded into the intersection. Suddenly he heard the scream of rubber. Too late he saw the silhouette of Jim's motorcycle careening head-on toward his car.

A split second later the impact separated Jim from his bike, throwing him through the air and into a concrete light post.

Two or three minutes later I drove up to the scene. In horror I immediately recognized the crumpled motorcycle and, not far from it, the bleeding body of my friend, Jim Harlan. A few minutes later I saw him being strapped onto a stretcher and lifted up into an ambulance, then rushed off toward the hospital.

I followed the ambulance to the hospital and waited there for word on Jim's condition. Many other people, Jim's family and friends, quickly arrived at the hospital. Some of us prayed together, and others just waited. What we didn't know then, but soon were told, was that Jim was already dead. He had been killed instantly in the collision.

I drove home that night choking on my tears, with two intense emotional forces warring within me: one, a black void, an abysmal sense of loss, as if something had been torn out of me and was forever gone; the other, a pounding, raging bitterness toward the man who had driven the car that had so senselessly, pointlessly ended the life of my friend who was so young, who had so many plans, who had so much to live for.

I wept long into that night.

The next morning I knew I had to go to the Harlans and offer what comfort I could. As I was walking to their house, the twin emotions of loss and bitterness welled up in me again, as potently as the night before. I remember thinking, *If I'm this bitter toward Mr. Smith, how must Mr. and Mrs. Harlan feel? Jim was my friend—but he was their only son.*

I arrived at the door and rang the bell. Mrs. Harlan answered the door and immediately embraced me. Tears streamed down her face.

The first words she said to me after she hugged me were quiet, spoken softly through her tears, but they went through me like a thunderbolt.

She said, "Do you know how Mr. Smith is doing? We've been praying for him so much since last night. You know, he's such an emotional person, and, well, we've just been praying that God would give him the strength to go through this terrible time."

I went inside and we sat down at the kitchen table. Mrs. Harlan began to share with me that even through this time of intense sorrow and grief, she had a sure sense of the love of Jesus Christ enfolding and comforting her, enabling her to show love and forgiveness toward Mr. Smith even in this horrible and unlovely situation.

We talked for a short time, and as I got up to leave she said, "When you see Mr. Smith, would you tell him something for us? Tell him that we love him, that we're praying for him."

I went outside, closed the door behind me, and leaned against the trunk of a big tree in the Harlans' front yard. With tears streaming down my face I asked Christ to come into my life in a new way. I asked Him to so infuse me with His Holy Spirit that I might be able to have the kind of love Mrs. Harlan had, the kind of love that would enable me to love and forgive in even the most unlovely situations in life.

God used the model of this woman's love to change my life. On that day I began to see that God was calling me as a catalyst to be used by God to help people learn to love each other with God's own kind of love. I don't believe this calling is unique to me. I believe that God through His Word has called *every* believer to be an agent of His love, His forgiveness, and His healing power.

We live in an unforgiving world, a world of sin and hatred

and anger. But we have a God of forgiveness, a heavenly Father who loves, accepts, and forgives us freely and unconditionally. The Father of forgiveness loved the world so much that He gave us His only Son, Jesus Christ, who taught us how to love, how to live, and how to *forgive*.

This kind of forgiving love is not just a sentiment or a feeling. It is a *power*—a power that my mother and father, both beautiful Christian people, began to teach me from the time I was old enough to understand.

It is a power that first really shook me and impressed me and began to redirect my life the day I saw it expressed through the death of an only son. Looking back, I'm amazed at how much Mrs. Harlan's forgiving love was patterned after that of another One who forgave the slaying of His only Son.

I'm still learning, day by day, about that power, about that forgiving love. I invite you to join me in a journey of discovery, as we learn together how to love, how to forgive, and how to be forgiven.

A New Kind of Love

The Bible has a lot to say about how God loves and forgives us, and how we are to love and forgive each other. First John 4:7-21 tells us that God didn't wait for us to change, to be sorry, or to take the first step. Rather, He demonstrated His all-enfolding, forgiving love toward us by taking the first step Himself, by reaching down to us and sending His Son as a sacrifice for our sin. God loves. God forgives. God reaches out to us first, even while we are still alienated from Him.

In his famous Love Chapter, Paul says this about love: "Love is patient, love is kind. It does not envy, it does not boast, it is not proud. It is not rude, it is not self-seeking, it is not easily angered, *it keeps no record of wrongs*. Love does not delight in evil but rejoices with the truth. It always protects, always trusts, always hopes, always perseveres. Love never fails. . . . And now these three remain: faith, hope and love. But the greatest of these is love.''[1]

In my home and in my church, all through my early life, I heard a lot about Christian love and forgiveness. But until the death of my friend, Jim Harlan, I never really understood what God's love, Christian love, the love that is described so beautifully in 1 Corinthians 13 and throughout the New Testament, is really all about. It was perplexing to me. It made no practical sense.

Jesus clearly commanded us to love our enemies.[2] As I was growing up, this sounded to me like an admirable ideal, but hardly practical.

How is it conceivable that I could feel nice, caring, warm feelings toward someone who is opposing me, abusing me, lying about me, making me miserable? How can one possibly feel *love* and *forgiveness* toward an enemy?

Perhaps that has been your conception of what the Bible means by the word "love." Nothing could be further from the truth. Love, as it is defined in these passages of the Bible, has nothing to do with warm, syrupy feelings of affection. In fact, it has nothing to do with our *feelings* at all! According to the Bible, Christian love—which is denoted in the original Greek New Testament by the word *agape*—is unconditional. It is rooted in the will. *It is a choice that we make, not an emotion that we experience.*

Jim Harlan's mother knew that. She demonstrated this kind of love when she freely forgave the man who had taken her son's life. She modeled that kind of love for me when she said to me, "Do you know how Mr. Smith is doing? When you see him, would you tell him that we love him, that we're praying for him?" I know that Mrs. Harlan was not filled with warm feelings; she was filled with the kind of pain and grief that only a bereaved parent can know.

But she made a *choice* to demonstrate a kind of love that is rooted in the will, a will that is surrendered over completely to God.

This is what the apostle Paul means when he says that love "is not self-seeking, it is not easily angered, it keeps no record of wrongs.... Love never fails."[3] Feelings are variable. Emotions change. But the kind of love that God has commanded us to demonstrate to other people *never* fails.

This *new* kind of love, which is rooted in an obedient will, is patient and kind, and is not self-seeking or easily angered. Emotionally-based forms of love, such as the romantic love between a man and a woman, cannot make such claims. Romantic love is all too often passionately impatient and self-seeking, quickly turning to anger and jealousy when wronged.

This *new* kind of love rejoices with the truth, never keeps track of wrongs, and always perseveres. But so-called "brotherly love" is good only so long as warm, brotherly feelings are present. "Brotherly love" can fail in the face of anger or rivalry. When betrayed, it can turn into bitterness.

This *new* kind of love does not boast, is not proud, is not self-seeking, and never fails. How unlike this kind of love is our craving for attention and approval and adulation! Some of us are trying to earn the approval of our family and friends; others are trying to get the attention of the world through fame and achievement.

The kind of love we need is the kind that accepts us as we are, the kind that never fails and never changes, whether we achieve greatly or fail greatly.

Before our family moved to the West Coast, I had the privilege for six years of serving as the Bible teacher for the Minnesota Vikings. During that time I observed over and over that one of the most traumatic times in any professional football player's life is when he starts to lose his quickness, his agility, his stamina. His career is coming to an end, and also, he realizes, are the love, praise, and adulation of his fans. A player often goes through a time of depression as he realizes he has been victimized by conditional love, that many of the people who said they cared—his fans, his teammates, and his coaches—didn't really care at all.

Conditional love fails. God's totally new kind of love—unconditional love—*never* fails.

What sets this new kind of love apart from all other forms

of love is that it is primarily a *self-sacrificing commitment of the will.* All other kinds of love, as beautiful as they may be, are essentially instinctive, emotional, temporal, and conditional. God has offered us this new kind of love, and He has commanded us to practice it toward other people. It's the only kind of love that's worthy of the name.

Learning the Hard Way

When the writers of the original Greek New Testament wanted to write about this new kind of love, the unconditional love of God, they found that they had no word in the Greek language to describe it. They had words for romantic love and family love and brotherly love, but God's unconditional love was something so radically new that there was no word that fit. So the New Testament writers appropriated the Greek word *agape*—a word that was so obscure that it can be found in only four places in all of classical Greek literature—and they gave this word a new and profound meaning.

Unconditional love is a necessary component of true, Christlike forgiveness. Free-flowing forgiveness is one expression of unconditional love. Where love and forgiveness are found, acceptance and wholeness and encouragement are found.

A lot of what I now understand about unconditional love I've had to learn the hard way, through finding out how conditional and unchristlike my own love toward other people has been.

I remember one young man named Tom who came into my counseling office. The last time I had seen him was a few years earlier when I was a youth pastor and he was one of the young people in our church. Tom told me that when he was in our youth group, he had a sense that my love and acceptance of him were in direct proportion to how committed he seemed to be to Christ.

He said to me, "You know, Ron, when I was deeply committed to Christ, when I had a great love for the Lord, when I was involved in Bible study and other programs at the church, you were my friend. You invited me to your apartment for Cokes and TV. We played tennis together. But when I began to drift away from the church, when I began to use drugs, when I got involved in the wrong activities with the wrong friends, it just seemed like we weren't *really* friends after all. When I really needed you, you weren't there.''

I knew Tom was right. My love for him had been conditional. I loved him as long as he conformed to my standards of Christian behavior. When his behavior fell below those standards— when, in fact, he needed my love and friendship the most—my love for him failed. "Love," wrote Paul, "*never* fails."

During the height of the Vietnam War, there was a record that was number one on all the charts for some 12 weeks. Entitled "An Open Letter To My Teenage Son," this record sold millions of copies, which should give you some sense of how popular this message was during those divisive times. With patriotic music and the roll of snare drums in the background, a father reads a letter he has written to his son.

In the letter he tells his son how lovingly he remembers the years when he was growing up, and how much he loves him now.

Just before this father reads the final line of this moving, stirring, loving letter, the music suddenly stops—and into the silence that follows he says: "But, son, if you burn your draft card, I no longer have a son." That's conditional love, love that fails.

God forgives. God loves. His love *never* fails.

Nowhere in His Word does God say, "I love you *if*. . ." Over and over He tells us, "I love you," *period*. Paul wrote in Romans, "God demonstrates his own love for us in this: While we were still sinners, Christ died for us."[4]

"Tell Her I Love Her"

Next to Calvary itself, the greatest story of unconditional love in the Bible is found in the Old Testament book of Hosea. This book has often been called the Gospel of John of the Old Testament, because of its emphasis on unconditional love—a kind of forgiving love the world doesn't understand.

The prophet Hosea was married to a prostitute. It isn't hard to imagine the abuse and ridicule that must have been heaped upon Hosea as, in obedience to God, he preached the gospel of repentance and forgiveness to the people of Israel.

Picture Hosea preaching, and a heckler stands and mocks him: "Hosea! Do you know what your wife is doing while you're here preaching to us 'sinners'? Do you know who she was with last night?"

What would Hosea reply? I suspect he would silence the heckler with words like these: "When you see her, would you tell her I love her?" That's unconditional love.

Notice what Hosea writes: "The Lord said to me, 'Go, show your love to your wife again, though she is loved by another and is an adulteress. Love her as the Lord loves the Israelites, though they turn to other gods.'"[5]

And that is what Hosea did—not because he naturally felt a warm affection for the woman who was unfaithful to him. He loved her by an obedient act of the will. He took the brokenness of his own painful marriage to an unfaithful wife, and turned it into a powerful analogy of God's love for you and me.

You may have been unfaithful to Jesus Christ this week. You may have been living in overt disobedience. But no matter what you have done, God wants you to know He loves you unconditionally and completely.

Love in Action

Rob and Sandy are dear friends of our family. One night a few short years ago Sandy was home alone. Rob was away on a business trip. The children were spending the night with friends.

That night Sandy heard a knock on the door. She asked who it was, and a man answered that his car broke down, that he needed to use the phone. Sandy let him in.

Instead of moving toward the phone, he advanced toward her, telling her he intended to rape her. She began to fight him off, and finally broke loose, lunging out the front door of their home. Screaming for help, she ran onto the front lawn. The man followed, cursing. He whipped out a gun, leveled it at Sandy, and pulled the trigger several times. Sandy fell, shot twice in the back. She crawled agonizingly to the street and collapsed as the neighbors began to come out of their homes, startled by the gunfire. Someone called an ambulance, and she was soon rushed to the hospital.

The man got away.

Within an hour, scores of people around the country were praying for Sandy as she struggled for her life. Her doctors didn't give her a good chance to live, and if she lived, they said, she would probably never walk again.

Today she is alive and able to walk. It's a beautiful miracle of healing. But there's yet another miracle of healing to this story.

I was talking to Rob not many months after this happened, and I was telling him how hard it was for me to love people who consciously sought to hurt me, who were willfully placing obstacles and trials in my way. And Rob began to tell me what had happened to the man who shot his wife.

He was captured, tried, convicted, and sentenced to prison. And during the process of that trial, God did a miracle of healing in the hearts of my friends, Rob and Sandy. After this man was committed to prison, Rob and Sandy went there and visited a number of times with this man. They shared Christ with him, and there have been growing indications that he is beginning to open his life to Christ.

That's unconditional love. It's *foolishness* to the world—but it's the foolishness of God that confounds the wisdom of men.

Unconditional love doesn't have anything to do with the way we feel. Hosea couldn't have felt too loving toward his unfaithful wife. Rob didn't feel too loving toward the man who had tried to rape and kill his wife. Unconditional love is rooted not in emotions but in the *will*, in our commitment to Christ, in allowing Christ to empower us so that we can love others as He has loved us: volitionally, unconditionally, with no strings attached.

God loves us unconditionally. God forgives us freely. May we show this same kind of love and forgiveness toward the people around us.

2

God Forgets

Bruce Larson tells the true story of a Catholic priest living in the Philippines, a much-beloved man of God who once carried a secret burden of long-past sin buried deep in his heart. He had committed that sin once, many years before, during his time in seminary. No one else knew of this sin. He had repented of it and he had suffered years of remorse for it, but he still had no peace, no inner joy, no sense of God's forgiveness.

There was a woman in this priest's parish who deeply loved God, and who claimed to have visions in which she spoke with Christ, and He with her. The priest, however, was skeptical of her claims, so to test her visions he said to her, "You say you actually speak directly with Christ in your visions. Let me ask you a favor. The next time you have one of these visions, I want you to ask Him what sin your priest committed while he was in seminary.''

The woman agreed and went home. When she returned to the church a few days later, the priest said, ''Well, did Christ visit you in your dreams?''

''Yes, He did,'' she replied.

''And did you ask Him what sin I committed in seminary?''

''Yes, I asked Him.''

''Well, what did He say?''

''He said, 'I don't remember.' ''

That is what God wants you to know about the forgiveness He freely offers you. When your sins are forgiven, they are *forgotten*. The past—with its sins, hurts, brokenness, and self-recrimination—is gone, dead, crucified, remembered no more.

What God forgives, He forgets.

A New Creation

''If anyone is in Christ,'' wrote Paul, ''he is a new creation; the old has gone, the new has come!''[6] How do you become a new creation in Christ? How can you know for sure that your sins are not only forgiven, but *forgotten*, exactly as if they had never happened?

We know God loves us unconditionally, and that He has made it possible for us to be forgiven and reconciled to Himself. Yet there is still a step that *we* must take in our own initiative in order to complete the process of reconciliation, to restore a right relationship with God, and to become new creations in Him. We must commit ourselves to His Son, Jesus Christ.

What does it mean to ''commit'' ourselves to Him? It means that we respond to the unconditional love He has shown us, recognizing that we are sinful and fall short of the kind of holy life He wants for us; that we turn away from our sins; and that we begin—through prayer, reading His Word, and fellowshipping with other Christians—to cultivate a *personal, daily relationship* with Jesus Christ.

From my own experience, I can say that *nothing* in the world is as important to me as my friendship with Jesus Christ. Knowing Him personally as Savior, as Friend, as Lord of my life, has enabled me to experience His forgiveness and unconditional love in my life. In turn, I find I'm beginning to know what it means to share that forgiving love with other people.

From the Scriptures and from my daily walk with God, I've grown to understand that being personally committed to Christ does not just mean giving mental assent to the right religious creed, or affirming a doctrinal statement, or being baptized at some time in life. As defined in the Bible, being a forgiven follower of Jesus Christ means nothing less than having a *relationship* with the living God of the universe. It means having complete access to God through prayer, so that I can go to Him with my failures, my faults, and even my worst sins, and always know that I will find complete acceptance and forgiveness.

God knows you completely and loves you completely, even though He knows you at your worst. With God, you are free to be you. You don't need to make any pretense of righteousness. He knows you and forgives you freely.

But while God's forgiveness is free, it isn't cheap. We should never treat His forgiveness as something to take lightly, to trample underfoot. God loves us so much that He wants much more for us than to simply escape punishment for our sins. He wants us to have a vital, daily *relationship* with Himself, and through that relationship He wants us to grow in character and maturity to be like His Son, Jesus Christ.[7] That is God's goal for our lives, and it must be our goal, too.

In order to achieve that goal of mature, Christlike character, we need to live a life of continual refreshment, renewal, and repentance—that is, turning away from the sins in which we used to live, and turning toward God.

Repentance doesn't mean promising God that we will never sin again as long as we live. We know, and God knows, that as long as we live we will be subject to sin. What it *does* mean is that we no longer see ourselves as given over to our sins; we no longer accept our sins as a normal component of our lives.

Rather, the new goal of our lives is to live a life of righteousness, and when we fall short of that goal, God will always be there to accept us and forgive us and encourage us to get up and try again.

Sincere repentance is a form of spiritual recycling, taking the dross and sin of our lives and transforming it into *refreshment* and *forgiveness* from God. "Repent, then, and turn to God, so that your sins may be wiped out, that times of refreshing may come from the Lord."[8]

Moreover, repentance is an active sign of our commitment to Christ. Paul tells us, "I preached that they should repent and turn to God and prove their repentance by their deeds."[9] All of us, at one time or another, have felt a vague spiritual uneasiness, a nameless feeling that all is not well with our souls.

I affirm the words of Luis Palau in his insightful booklet *Experiencing God's Forgiveness*: "I don't believe the Holy Spirit leaves us guessing when He reveals sin in our lives. Satan, on the other hand, is the master of causing us to feel a generalized sense of guilt and unworthiness."[10]

It's Satan's job to make us feel unforgiven and unacceptable to God. Sometimes we make Satan's job easy for him by failing to live a life of free-flowing repentance and refreshing forgiveness. When we feel a vague sense of spiritual disquiet, it's good to consider whether we are truly living a life of repentance. If not, then we have *forgotten* that we've been cleansed from our past sins,[11] and that uneasy feeling is probably Satan's attempt—made possible by the foothold we've given him—to make us feel unworthy and unaccepted by God.

But when we live a life of cleansing repentance, we know our sins are forgiven, we become increasingly assured of our salvation, and Satan can't make us doubt our Father-child relationship with God.

Spiritual Breathing

God intends that repentance and forgiveness should be the

spiritual air we breathe. Exhale: repentance. Inhale: forgiveness. The Christian who has a continuing, constantly-regenerating sense of God's acceptance and forgiveness is *free*—free to live boldly and courageously for Christ, free to love and forgive others, free to be used by God in great and powerful ways.

Are there sins in your life that you can't forget, memories of past sins that hold you back from feeling forgiven and accepted and loved by God?

If so, then God wants you to know that the past sin that is weighing you down has been put to death, crucified on the cross of Jesus Christ. The sacrifice of Christ on Calvary was so incalculably precious and so rich in merit that it abundantly, lavishly covers even the blackest, most unspeakable sins—blots them out completely and forever!

If you have accepted the free gift of His forgiveness, if you have committed yourself to Christ, then He has not only forgiven your sin, but He has *forgotten* it! He's given you His Word on it: "As far as the east is from the west, so far has he removed our transgressions from us."[12]

How far is the east from the west? If you are a follower of Jesus Christ, a child of God, that's how far removed you stand right now from *every sin you ever committed*! If you have sincerely repented of your sin and committed your life to Christ, and yet you still carry a burden of guilt for the past, then that's a needless burden of guilt.

Imagine—the all-knowing God of the universe promises to *forget*! He tells us, "Their sins and lawless acts I will remember no more."[13]

What do we do with that promise? How do we appropriate it for our lives? How do we come to trust God's promise to forgive us and forget our past sins?

The apostle Paul has the answer to these questions: "Forgetting what is behind and straining toward what is ahead, I press on toward the goal to win the prize for which God has called me heavenward in Christ Jesus."[14]

We need to quit looking back, quit dwelling in the past, quit listening to the Accuser, Satan, who is trying to convince us that the sins of our past have ended our hopes for the future. *Forget what is behind.*

But even more, we must mobilize, fix our eyes on God, the Father of love and forgiveness, and strain ahead toward the glorious, exalted future He has planned for us. God is calling you heavenward in Christ Jesus, so *press on* toward the goal! Press on in faith and obedience and trust in His promise to you: The past is done with; our sins are forgiven and forgotten; He remembers them no more.

You are not held accountable for the sins of the past anymore. Today you are responsible for today. Take today and live it for the glory of God.

_____ **3**

Forgiving Yourself

Julie was an attractive, sensitive, outgoing young woman about 19 years of age. Though she had been reared in a Christian home, she had made some wrong choices in her life, and now she faced the consequences of those choices. Julie found herself pregnant by a man who had abandoned her rather than take responsibility for the child they had made. As a result, Julie had a load of guilt and self-reproach that wouldn't go away.

Seeking counsel and a sense of forgiveness and relief from her feelings of guilt, Julie tried to talk to her mother. But Julie's mother broke into tears whenever Julie tried to bring up the subject of her pregnancy. It was clear she couldn't talk to her mother about this.

She talked to a few of her friends. They assured her that "Everybody's doing it. You just got caught, that's all." But when

Julie pressed her friends further, asking what she could do about this terrible guilt she was carrying, they could only shrug and say, "Gee, Julie, I don't know what to tell you."

Feeling more isolated, more alone, more unforgiven than ever, Julie consulted a psychiatrist. "Your problem is nothing new or unusual," he told her. "You were raised in a very religious home, and these unattainably high moral standards were imposed on you from your childhood. You became sexually involved with a man, which is only natural for a woman of your age. When you became pregnant, your lifelong religious conditioning began to beat you down, make you feel guilty, make you feel as though you had 'sinned.' I can help you. We'll work together on these guilt feelings, and soon we'll begin to free you from all these moral commitments, these religious standards and judgmental restrictions that are holding back your emotional growth."

Julie took her psychiatrist's advice. She continued to meet with him and talk to him, and over the weeks she gradually began to feel better. She found she was able to push her guilt down, repress it, and hide it out of sight for the remainder of her pregnancy.

Finally Julie gave birth to a beautiful baby boy, and she named him Stephen. She loved and cherished that little boy more than anything else in the world. She enjoyed buying him clothes and dressing him up in different outfits. She read all the books she could find on childcare, child-rearing, and mother-child nutrition. She wanted her little Stephen to get the best start in life he could possibly have.

One day a neighbor woman stopped by Julie's apartment for a visit. As she walked up the steps, she noticed that the front door was ajar. She pushed the door open and called, "Julie?" She heard a sound from inside like someone sobbing—but there was no reply. She stepped into the darkened living room, and as her eyes adjusted to the gloom she was shaken with horror at what she saw. "Julie!" she cried. "What are you doing?"

There, kneeling on the floor, was Julie, looking rumpled and disheveled, her hair falling over her tear-streaked face—and her hands tightly gripping little Stephen's neck in a choke hold.

"Julie, let go!" the neighbor commanded firmly, reaching down and prying Julie's fingers from the baby's throat. The baby slumped out of Julie's grip and lay in Julie's lap, very still and very quiet.

A heartbeat passed.

Then little Stephen gasped for breath—and began to cry. The neighbor woman had prevented the little boy's death by only a few seconds.

Why did Julie try to take the life of the beautiful little child she loved so much? Even Julie herself didn't know.

She was referred to a Christian counselor, who began to help her uncover the reasons for her actions. Together they began to discover that the guilt that the psychiatrist had urged Julie to repress and deny and bury was still there, festering and growing and poisoning her spirit from deep within.

The attempt she had made against her baby's life was really an attempt to punish *herself*, by destroying her most precious and cherished possession. In her hidden guilt and self-reproach, there was a secret part of herself that believed she could never deserve such a beautiful gift from God as this baby.

Through a long, difficult, painful process of squarely facing her guilt, and of learning about the all-forgiving, all-accepting, unconditional love of God the Father, Julie came to be healed in her spirit. She was finally able to forgive herself. Today she is married to a loving, understanding Christian man who has adopted Stephen, and together they are raising this little boy for the Lord.

We all need to learn the lesson that Julie learned. We need to know the cleansing love and forgiveness of God, and we need to learn to *forgive ourselves*.

Not Okay, But Forgiven

What does it mean to "forgive ourselves"? Many people would say that it means that we agree together that "I'm okay, you're okay." This is essentially what the psychiatrist wanted Julie to do: She should set aside the unhealthy "religious conditioning" and those "moral standards" and simply realize that she was "okay" as she was.

The trouble was, Julie wasn't okay. She had sinned, and there was a part of herself deep down that *knew* she had sinned. With the help of her psychiatrist, Julie was able to rationalize her guilt, and she actually felt better for a while. But what she was missing was a true and cleansing sense of *forgiveness*.

Being told she was "okay" was nothing more than a psychiatric Band-Aid over a gangrenous wound of guilt. What she needed—and what God finally enabled her to find—was a truly *healing* sense of forgiveness. And forgiveness only comes as we *face* the truth of our sins, not in repressing or denying that truth.

Julie's problem was not that she had an exaggerated view of her sins, not that her guilt was out of proportion to her sin. No, the fact is that the burden on her conscience was probably fairly accurate. Her sin, which happened to be in the area of sexual temptation, was certainly no worse than the sins that are common to us all. But she had sinned, and she incurred the consequences of sin—guilt and a sense of condemnation.

What *was* out of proportion was her view of God and His love and forgiveness. Julie's picture of God was incomplete. She was aware of His standard of righteousness, but was unable to focus on His overwhelming forgiveness and acceptance of her. She failed to see that the precious sacrifice of Jesus Christ on the cross was vastly, abundantly, overwhelmingly rich and ample to cover even the deepest, blackest sins anyone has ever committed. And because she was unable to trust the sacrifice of Christ to cover her sins, she felt a need to bear the punishment for her sins herself.

That is the tragedy of so many of us as Christians: The price of *all* our sins has been paid by Jesus at Calvary, and yet we still feel we must pay for our sins ourselves.

In Europe in the thirteenth century, during the time of the Black Plague, there was a fanatical cult called the Flagellants. This cult, which became a widespread heretical sect of Christianity in the Middle Ages, held long and loud processions through the cities of Europe in which they walked naked, beating themselves with whips and chains and rods until their bodies were lacerated and bleeding.

Why? Because they believed that unless they themselves suffered cruelly and miserably for their sins, they could not be forgiven.

We may look back at such practices and shake our heads, thinking, "How senseless! Didn't they know why Christ went to the cross? Couldn't they see that He took our sins on Himself so that we wouldn't have to bear the punishment for those sins ourselves?"

And yet *we* do the same thing today! Many of us are twentieth century Flagellants, flogging ourselves for sins that God has already forgiven—*and forgotten*! We continue to beat ourselves down emotionally and mentally for sins that we have already confessed and repented of and seen crucified years ago. It is as if we are telling Christ, "You died for nothing. My sin is still with me, and nothing—not even Your death on the cross—will ever take it away!"

Is this what you are telling Christ today? Is this your view of God and His forgiveness? If you believe your sins are too great for God to forgive, then your God is too small! The true, living God of the Bible offers grace upon grace upon grace, and His grace is greater than *all* our sins!

Grace: There's Got to Be a Catch!

Perhaps the thing that is holding you back from forgiving yourself is that you haven't grasped the meaning and extent of God's unconditional love and grace toward you. You've failed to fully grasp the rich, exultant truth of Ephesians 2:4,5: "Because of his *great love* for us, God, who is *rich in mercy*, made us alive with Christ even when we were dead in transgressions—it is *by grace* you have been saved." Or the resounding assurance of John 1:16: "From the *fullness of his grace* we have all received *one blessing after another*."

Grace is a difficult concept for almost all of us. We can't seem to get it through our heads and into our hearts that God's forgiveness really is *free and overwhelmingly vast*. There's got to be a catch. Somewhere in this process we have some dues to pay, right?

Wrong. Paul says, "For it is *by grace* you have been saved, through faith—and this not from yourselves, it is the *gift of God— not by works*, so that no one can boast."[15] There is nothing you need to do to earn God's forgiveness; indeed there is nothing you *can* do to earn it. It's quite simply a gift of grace, and there are only two options in regard to a gift: Accept it or reject it. You cannot "earn" a gift.

Paul goes on in the next verse to tell us that we are God's handcrafted workmanship, created through Christ's saving work on the cross to do good works.[16] Notice that those good works can't earn for us God's forgiveness; the preceding verses have already made that clear.

Rather the free gift of God's abundant grace has *liberated* us to do the good works we were created to do. And we do them not to "earn" God's forgiveness, but out of a heart of gratitude for the fact that He has *already* freely forgiven us.

Grace is such a simple idea. In fact, it's probably the sheer simplicity of grace that makes it so hard for us to grasp and appropriate God's grace for our own lives. We just can't believe that forgiveness is offered to us freely, graciously, at no charge to us. But it's true! We are no longer debtors to God because of our sin; our account is marked PAID IN FULL.

Dealing with Guilt

In order to be effectively used by God, we have to *know* we're forgiven. We have to have a clean conscience. The writer to the Hebrews tells us that it is the sacrifice of Christ that can abundantly "cleanse our consciences from acts that lead to death, so that we may serve the living God."[17] Clearly, the Christian who does not have a cleansed conscience will be held back in his service toward the living God.

How can we have a clean conscience?

For the Christian the problem is one of perspective. We need to see ourselves as God sees us. We need to recognize that the basis of a clean conscience is not ignoring or denying our sin, but the knowledge that our sin has been covered, blotted out of God's sight, by the infinite sacrifice of Jesus Christ.

If we want to feel cleansed, whole, and forgiven, we must begin by squarely facing the awful truth of our sin. This is a painful process, and our first inclination is to shrink from it. We would rather think positively about ourselves. We would rather compare ourselves to someone else and say, "I'm really not *that* bad compared to him, compared to her." We would rather be labeled "okay" than find true healing and honest forgiveness.

There may be another reason you don't feel forgiven. Perhaps you actually *have* faced the awfulness of your sin. And in accepting that realization, you have also accepted an idea that you can never be free of that guilt. Perhaps there are specific sins in your past that continue to beat you down and make you feel unworthy. You've confessed them and repented of them, but the guilt won't leave you alone.

The clear, unequivocal promise of Scripture is that Jesus Christ died to free us from our guilt, to separate us forever from the weight and accusation of our sin. Why, then, do so many of us feel so defeated by guilt? First, I believe we need to clarify what we mean by guilt. Sometimes we loosely use the word "guilt" to refer to two very different things:

1) *The conviction of sin* that the Holy Spirit brings, which He uses to guide us toward repentance and forgiveness. This is *short-term* guilt. God never intends that we should be haunted by this kind of guilt for years and years; rather, He wants us to respond to the Holy Spirit's conviction, to repent, and to be restored to wholeness and a joyful relationship with Him.

2) *The accusation of Satan*. Satan will sometimes beat us down and make us feel guilty over sins that have been forgiven and forgotten by God years and years ago. According to Revelation

12:10, Satan is the Accuser of every Christian. It's his job to try to discredit the faith and righteousness of each believer by jabbing an accusing finger at that believer's sin. He is like a prosecutor in a court of law.

But God assures us that we have the best Defense Attorney in the universe: "If anybody does sin, we have one who speaks to the Father in our defense—Jesus Christ, the Righteous One."[18] When guilt over a confessed, repented, forgiven sin comes back to haunt you, then claim the truth of 1 John 2:1, and stamp that acccusation RETURN TO SENDER! Remember, as a child of God, you're not guilty—you're *forgiven*! God forgives you and *forgets* your sin.

Closely related to the sense of guilt that comes through the accusation of Satan is the feeling of guilt that comes through the accusation and judgments of other people. In some cases their accusation and judgment may be factually accurate; they point the finger of guilt at us over some sin we actually committed, but have repented of and have been forgiven of by God. In other cases, people may accuse us falsely, or judge our motives, or blame us for circumstances that were beyond our control. In either case, whether we are completely forgiven or completely innocent, there will always be people around trying to make us feel guilty; there will always be self-appointed judges and critics.

What can you do about it? What *should* you do about it? The answer to both questions: Nothing. You can't please everyone, convince everyone, justify yourself before everyone. You shouldn't even try.

Paul said, "Am I now trying to win the approval of men, or of God? . . . If I were still trying to please men, I would not be a servant of Christ."[19] The only opinion of us that we need be concerned about is God's—and if He forgives us, it's the same as if we were innocent. When we *know* with assurance that we are righteous in God's sight, then what other people think doesn't matter at all.

When others condemn you falsely, or judge you for something that God has forgiven and forgotten, then you can look them in the eye and say with rock-steady assurance, "You're free to think whatever you want. That's your problem, not mine. According to God, I'm forgiven, and His is the only opinion that matters to me."

George Whitefield (1714-1770), the great English evangelist and man of God, once received a letter that spitefully accused him of assorted wrongs in his ministry. Whitefield returned a brief, courteous reply that stands as an example to anyone who is judged and accused by others: "I thank you heartily for your letter," he wrote. "As for what you and my other enemies are saying against me, I know worse things about myself than you will ever say about me. With love in Christ, George Whitefield."

That is the response of a man who seeks to please God, not men.

There is only one kind of guilt feeling that we should pay any attention to: the conviction of sin by the Holy Spirit. That conviction comes to us sharply focused on specific sins, and it has a positive, short-term purpose. Our response should be to confess that sin, repent of it, and get on with the business of living a forgiven life through the power of the Holy Spirit.

When you live a life of free-flowing confession and repentance from your sins, God will faithfully, continually forgive you. He will liberate you from the oppression of guilt and the accusation of Satan. Then you will be *free*—free to truly live, to truly forgive others, to truly forgive yourself.

4

The Past Is Over

I once counseled a woman who had recently come to know Jesus Christ as her Savior and Lord. Before she committed herself to Christ, this woman had been involved in a long succession of unhappy affairs with different men. She had come to Christ with many painful memories and a heavy weight of sin, and God was enabling her, over a period of time, to renew her mind and release her from the guilt of her past.

One day the realization of God's complete forgiveness and forgetfulness of her past sins broke in on her heart like a healing flood of light. "I've just discovered something *wonderful* about myself!" she beamed joyfully. "I just realized that today, in God's sight, I am a virgin!"

This woman was absolutely right: The past—with its sins, guilt, and hurts—is over, forgotten, dead, and buried. She is now *free*—free to live the kind of rich, bold, abundant life that God wants for every believer. He wants us to live the kind of lives that reach out to others in reconciling love, lives which dare grand and adventurous things for His glory. He wants us to be free to eagerly serve Him; free to continually share His love with others; free to feel clean and forgiven and blameless.

In order to live the way God intends us to live, we need a clean conscience, a pure heart. We need to have God's perspective on our sin, on our past, and on His great, all-inclusive forgiveness and love toward us. We need to know that the past is over, that today we are responsible for *today*.

One man who sinned greatly, but who was able to gain God's perspective on his life by facing his sin, was the psalmist David. Many words have been written and many sermons have been preached about David the Shepherd Boy, or David the King, or David the Man After God's Own Heart. But we tend to gloss over one of the dark stains on David's past. We tend to pass quickly by the story of David the Murderer and Adulterer. But by taking a closer look at the scandal of King David, I believe we can learn some profound truths for our own lives about the abundant forgiveness of God.

It may seem paradoxical, but I find great encouragement and consolation in the fact that the Scriptures include the sins and failures of God's people as well as their triumphs. People like David are presented in the Bible exactly as they were—flesh and blood like you and I—not larger-than-life, perpetually victorious legends and heroes.

I find that fact encouraging because 1) it offers evidence of the reliability and integrity of the Bible, in that it presents the truth, not a whitewash, of the lives of God's people; and 2) it depicts people with whom we can identify, people who are like us—prone to failure, prone to sin, prone to let God down. If I can see God in the act of forgiving David for his sins, giving him another chance, then I can trust Him to forgive my sins as well.

Second Samuel chapters 11 and 12 tells how King David's sin begins with his adulterous thoughts toward Bathsheba, the wife of Uriah. David's next step, then, is to act on his thoughts: He commits adultery with Bathsheba.

When Bathsheba becomes pregnant, David hatches different plots to prevent Uriah from discovering his sin. He ultimately goes so far as to send Uriah to the front lines of a fierce battle, whereupon he orders the soldiers around Uriah to "withdraw from him so he will be struck down and die." The order is carried out, and Uriah is killed just as David had planned. David then takes Uriah's widow into his own house, where she bears him a son.

"But," the Scriptures say, "the thing David had done displeased the Lord."[20]

The Lord sends the prophet Nathan to David. Nathan confronts David with the depth of his sin, saying, "Why did you despise the word of the Lord by doing what is evil in His eyes?"[21]

When David hears Nathan's stinging rebuke, he is filled with grief and remorse. "I have sinned against the Lord,"[22] he groans.

Then Nathan testifies to the abundant forgiveness of God: that though David's sinful actions will have hard consequences in this world, nevertheless "the Lord has taken away your sin."[23]

The Lord's forgiveness toward David is free and abundant, predicated not on any good works of David but simply upon his confession and repentance. David's grateful response to God for His forgiveness is recorded in Psalm 51, David's psalm of confession and repentance. The words of this psalm come from the heart of one who has found God's perspective on his past sins:

> Have mercy on me, O God,
>   according to your unfailing love;
> according to your great compassion
>   blot out my transgressions.
> Wash away all my iniquity
>   and cleanse me from my sin. . . .
>
> Cleanse me with hyssop, and I will be clean;
>   wash me, and I will be whiter than snow. . . .
> Hide your face from my sins
>   and blot out all my iniquity.

> Create in me a pure heart, O God,
> and renew a steadfast spirit within me.[24]

Even though David committed heinous sins that most of us would shudder to even contemplate, God *forgave* David and *used* him for His glory. Ultimately God pronounced this praise upon him: "My servant David...kept my commands and followed me with all his heart, doing only what was right in my eyes."[25]

Does this sound like the description of a murderer, of an adulterer? Of course not! But this was *God's perspective* on the life of David—not because David was innocent, but because he was *forgiven*. His past sins were covered, blotted out, forgotten. And if God can forgive and forget the crimes of David, He can forgive your sins as well.

The prayer of David should be your prayer and mine: "Lord, please have mercy on me! Blot out my sins! Wash me, cleanse me, pour Your love and forgiveness over me! Create in me a pure heart, a clean conscience!"

That *can* be your prayer. That *can* be your perspective on your sins, on your past life. You *can* forgive yourself.

Act on His Promise!

As we've seen, the Scriptures give us assurance upon assurance of God's cleansing forgiveness for the most unspeakable sins we have ever committed. As you continue to meditate daily in God's Word, I believe He will enable you to understand more and more fully the height and depth and breadth and tenderness of God's forgiving love for you.

At the same time, however, I'm convinced that you will *never* find complete healing in the area of self-acceptance and self-forgiveness by merely hearing or reading assurances of God's forgiveness toward you. I believe you need to be *challenged* to take responsibility for your own feelings, and to take *action* to assist God in His effort to make you whole.

Have you confessed your sinfulness to God? Have you made a sincere commitment of repentance for your sins? Have you asked God to forgive you and cleanse you from your sin? Then you need to stand up and be a man of God or a woman of God who *knows* you are forgiven!

The past is over. God *has* forgiven you! *Forgive yourself!*

Whatever we pray, we must commit ourselves to. An excellent example of this principle was the apostle Paul. In his preconversion past he had sinned greatly. Following his encounter with the risen Christ, Paul committed himself to forgiveness and being forgiven, and thus he was able to forgive himself, and God was able to use him in mighty ways.

Before his conversion to Christ, Paul was a ruthless, vengeful persecutor of Christians, an arrogant Pharisee who openly reviled the name of Jesus Christ. Throughout the New Testament Paul freely confesses, "I am the least of the apostles and do not even deserve to be called an apostle, because I persecuted the church of God";[26] "I was once a blasphemer and a persecutor and a violent man."[27]

But Paul could trust the love and acceptance and grace of God as being sufficient to cover the guilt of the worst sinner who ever lived—for that is precisely who Paul considered himself to have been. "Here is a trustworthy saying," wrote Paul to Timothy, "that deserves full acceptance: Christ Jesus came into the world to save sinners—of whom I am the worst. But for that very reason I was shown mercy so that in me, the worst of sinners, Christ Jesus might display his unlimited patience as an example for those who would believe on him and receive eternal life."[28]

Do you see what Paul is saying? In essence, he is looking you right in the eye and saying, "There's *no* sin you've committed that God cannot forgive. If you don't believe it, then look at me! God redeemed me, the very worst of sinners, in order to prove to you that God can forgive *anyone*, no matter what they've done! I'm your example! I'm living proof of God's infinite patience and forgiveness toward you!"

If you have been unable to forgive yourself for some sin in

your past, or if you are feeling defeated by some struggle with sin that is going on in your life, then Paul would say to you, "The past is over. Forget what is behind. Move out into the future with your eyes fixed on God and His love. He's calling you heavenward in Christ, so *press on toward the goal!*"

God Isn't Through with You Yet

Insightful author/pastor John Claypool has written a powerfully instructive book called *The Light Within You*. There he tells the story of a man who had come to him, broken and guilt-ridden, seeking counseling, seeking some words that would enable him to forgive himself. In tears, in an agony of remorse and self-reproach, this man poured out his story to John Claypool.

One day this man had become involved in a bitter argument with his wife. The argument built to a point where he stormed angrily out of his house, jumped into his car, and began backing heedlessly down his driveway. The car suddenly lurched over something in the drive. The man hit the brakes—and discovered he had run over and killed his three-year-old son, who had followed him out of the house. "I shall never forget the horror on his face," writes Claypool, "as he told me about looking over the hood and seeing the body of his child in the driveway."[29]

What would you say to this man if you were in John Claypool's position? What words could you offer to make him feel healed of the guilt of having carelessly, senselessly slain his little boy? No words will ever bring his child back. Surely this man must feel that his own life is over, that his usefulness to God is ended, that there is nothing left in life but remorse and self-hate.

But this man's story wasn't over.

Through a long process of grief and tears, of learning from the Scriptures, and being supported emotionally and prayerfully by the brothers and sisters of his church family, this man came to a point where he could turn to God and let His forgiveness pour over his life and wash him completely clean.

And in gratitude for God's forgiveness, Claypool says that this man became "the mover in one of the most successful Boy Scout movements in all of the South, doing for other boys what he could never do for his own son. And he is not doing it, mind you, in order to earn God's mercy, but *because* that mercy was given."

Then Claypool concludes:

> It's important to realize that the efforts we make to repair the damage we have done and to undergo growth within ourselves are not something we do in order to earn forgiveness, but something we undertake *because we have been forgiven*. They are the consequences, not the conditions, of redemption; there is all the difference in the world between these fruits of forgiveness and our futile attempts at self-atonement.[30]

No matter what you've done, your story isn't over. God isn't through with you yet. He stands ready to forgive you, and to *transform* the consequences of your sins into something beautiful for your growth, for service toward others, and for His glory.

God, the Father of forgiveness, doesn't demand that you make your own atonement. He offers His gift freely of His own grace, on the infinite merit of His own crucified Son, Jesus. When you immerse yourself in His overflowing forgiveness, says Isaiah 1:18, your blood-scarlet, sin-stained life will become "as white as snow."

"As far as the east is from the west," says Psalm 103:12, "so far has he removed our transgressions from us."

"He is faithful and just and will forgive us our sins and purify us from all unrighteousness," assures 1 John 1:9.

And when we *feel* His forgiveness, and when we *know* He has cleansed and purified us, then we are free to live for Him, and He is able to use us.

If you have given your life to God, trusting in the sacrifice of Jesus Christ on the cross, then God *has* forgiven you. That's a truth you can commit your life to. If God has forgiven you, forgive yourself.

The past is over. Take *today* and live it for Him.

_____ **5**

Nothing to Fear

It was one of the best times in my life. I was 22 years old, just finishing my seminary studies, and dividing my weekends between two little Iowa churches—churches I remember fondly for their faithfulness to Christ and their caring for each other and for me.

Late one night I was driving back to my apartment. While I was driving I noticed a police car following me. As I drove, I kept an eye on the mirror. When I turned a corner, the police car turned too. I nervously checked my speedometer, wondered if my brake lights were working, tried to recall if I had used my turn indicator at the corner. Why would a police car be following *me*?

I turned another corner. The police car continued to follow. Its red lights began to flash and it accelerated alongside me. The policeman ordered me to the side of the road, and I complied.

I waited while the uniformed officer got out and strode up to my car. His tone was crisp and authoritative as he said, "Would you get out of the car, sir?"

I got out.

"You're the new preacher in town, aren't you?"

"Well, yes. I'm the pastor of the First Presbyterian Church here in town," I said.

"I've seen you hanging around some of the young punks in town."

"Well, I've been trying to get to know some of the young men at the high school—"

"Listen," he interrupted, "I've got some good advice for you. You shouldn't hang around those punks anymore. They're hoods, they're no good, they've been nothing but trouble to me. If you want to have a ministry in this town, you just stay away from those hoods."

There was no mistaking the implications of that "advice."

In the weeks that followed, I continued to get to know a number of these young men, these so-called "punks" and "hoods." It was one of the most rewarding experiences of my life. One of these that I befriended was a troubled young man named Ken.

Ken had indeed been in and out of trouble for a long time. As we visited together, I found that there was one big block in his heart and his mind that kept him from turning to God and accepting His cleansing and forgiveness. Ken would say to me, "Ron, you wouldn't believe the things I've done. I mean, if you knew all the sins I've committed, you wouldn't even be sitting here talking to me. God knows all about my past, and there's no way He can love me and forgive me for some of the rotten things I've done—no way."

I said, "Well, tell me what you've done."

He hesitated to even begin, but then he told me one thing, and then another, and soon a sordid tale of crime, sin, and degrading acts began to spill out.

But as I began to open the Scriptures to Ken, he began to see that God didn't require him to live up to His moral law. God's forgiveness is given by His *grace*, and it's received through our *faith*, as we commit ourselves to Jesus Christ as our Savior and Lord. We can't earn God's forgiveness; we can only accept it.

It was my joy and privilege to pray with Ken as he opened his heart to receive God's forgiveness. Today he is a follower of Jesus Christ.

Ken's problem is a common one. I know from the scores of people who have passed through my counseling room that there are vast numbers of people who cannot bring themselves to turn to God for salvation, fearing that their sins are too many or too grievous for God to ever accept them. And there are many Christians who wrestle with the fear that they are not truly forgiven, not truly accepted by God.

We need to understand what the Bible says about the character of God. We need to know and to feel that we truly have a God of forgiveness, a God of love, a God of unconditional acceptance. As we become healed in our image of God, we will begin to find healing in our relationship to God.

And what does the Bible say about the forgiving nature of God? "You are kind and forgiving, O Lord, abounding in love to all who call to you."[31]

We serve a God of forgiveness. This fact—once we have grasped it and seized it and made it a foundational truth in our lives—is a great comfort and assurance to us. But the joyous fact that God loves and accepts and forgives us does not negate the fact that there is something in our lives that needs to be dealt with, something called *sin*.

The Old Truths Versus the New Jargon

Many Christians today feel a little embarrassed to use such terms as *sin*, *guilt*, and *judgment*. These words sound a little old-fashioned, a bit too harsh, and perhaps even irrelevant to the psychological and sociological realities of twentieth-century man.

Our culture ridicules and belittles the terminology used by God's Word to describe the turbulence of the human condition, so when we say the word "sin," we often tend to feel a little foolish.

In the vernacular of our times, we don't commit sin; we "act out inappropriate behavior patterns." We don't carry a load of guilt; we are "victims of poor conditioning." We don't need to be forgiven; we need to be "reprogrammed" or "repatterned" in our thinking.

We've exchanged the truth of Scripture for a whole new lexicon of feel-good, nonjudgmental jargon from the human potential movement, est, TM, and dozens of other pop psychological and sociological movements, fads, and isms. But our situation is the same today as when the Bible was written: We *sin*, we carry the *guilt* of that sin, we incur the natural *consequences* of that sin, and we need to be *forgiven*.

The noted poet and critic T.S. Eliot describes this condition in *The Cocktail Party*. He presents a conversation between a woman named Celia and her psychiatrist, Dr. Reilly, regarding something that is troubling her, causing her a nagging sense of anxiety. "It sounds ridiculous," she says, "but the only word for it that I can find is a sense of *sin*."

Probing for the root cause of her "ridiculous" obsession with "sin," the doctor asks, "What is the point of view of your family?"

"Well," she replies, "my bringing up was pretty conventional—I had always been taught to disbelieve in sin. Oh, I don't mean that it was never mentioned! But anything wrong, from our point of view, was either bad form, or was psychological.... I don't see why mistakes should make one feel sinful! And yet I can't find any other word for it.... It's [a feeling] of emptiness, of failure towards someone, or something, outside of myself. And I feel I must...*atone*—is that the word? Can you treat a patient for such a state of mind?"[32]

We are sick. Our condition is serious, and needs appropriate treatment. We will never become well as long as we refuse to face the true nature of our illness.

Our illness is called *sin*.

The Consequences of Sin

I received a letter several years ago that brought tears to my eyes. It was written by a girl I met briefly while speaking at a conference on the East Coast. In the first part of her letter she told me a little more about herself than she had revealed when we met: She was a 17-year-old high school student who had become involved with a young man, had become pregnant by him, and had become desperate. She did not seek counsel from anyone, but chose during the second trimester of her pregnancy to have her baby aborted. She concluded:

> The problem, Dr. Davis, is that since I waited so long to make up my mind and get up enough nerve to have the abortion, there was some danger involved. I couldn't let my parents know about this, so I went ahead with it anyway. Now, because of that decision, I will be unable to have children in the future. I love children so much, and I've always wanted children of my own. Now I can't ever have them. I've ruined my chances. I just don't understand why God has put me through this.

There is no easy answer to the tragedy described in this letter. This young woman has made some very common, human mistakes in her life, but mistakes that nonetheless come under the category called *sin*. My heart went out to this young friend in her suffering and self-reproach. I know the heart of God was broken for her too.

In reply, I wrote and told her how God loves her exactly as she is, no matter what she has done; how He stands ready to forgive her and accept her freely; how He wants to use the trial she is going through to teach her about His love and grace, and to help her grow to become in character more like Jesus Christ.

But I also told her that the consequences of her wrong choices were real; she would not be able to change them. She was going to have to allow those consequences to *change her* in ways that would bring about growth, maturity, and Christlikeness in her life.

Many of us, when we sin and experience the natural consequences of our sin, begin to picture God as looking down upon us in anger, in vengeance, devising some suffering to punish us for our sin. This conception—or rather, this *mis*conception—is implied in my young friend's letter when she writes, "I just don't understand why God has put me through this."

What I told this young woman, and what you and I have to understand, is that God is not in the business of dealing vengeance and wrath to His own children. God hates sin, but He loves the sinner. God doesn't want to hurt us; He wants to heal us. Most of all, He wants to heal us of the devastating effects of sin.

The Scriptures continually, repeatedly, exultantly tell us about God's personal, gracious, fatherly *love* and *forgiveness* and *acceptance* and *faithfulness* toward us—but they *never* tell us that God personally directs anger or vengeance at His own children. How could He, when every sin we've ever committed has been forgiven and forgotten by God?

But many of us fall into the same trap my young friend did: We sin, knowing full well that there are risks and consequences associated with that sin; we incur the logical consequences of that sin; then we implore, "Why is God putting me through this?" Of course, it was not God but *we* who brought this misfortune upon *ourselves*.

God has established His universe with both a material order and a moral order. An example of the workings of the material order is the law of gravity. We may not like the law of gravity. We may disagree with it. We may choose not to believe in it. But our belief or lack of belief in it does not alter the fact that gravity operates in the material universe, part of the impersonal natural order established in the beginning by God.

If a man exercises his God-given free will and throws himself from the top of a tall building, we can be sure that he will incur some exceedingly unpleasant consequences upon his arrival on the pavement below.

Was God there *pushing* him off the building? Ridiculous! Is God angrily pulling him down to the pavement so as to hurt him and exact vengeance? Certainly not! This man exercised his own free will. He violated the natural order of the universe, and he incurred the reasonable, predictable, cause-and-effect consequences.

The moral order functions in much the same way. When we violate moral laws, we risk the reasonable, predictable, cause-and-effect consequences associated with that violation, but God is not directing His *personal* anger toward us at such moments.

Rather, God is *with* us, alongside us in the Person of the Holy Spirit, who patiently pleads with us in our conscience to turn aside from our sin; in the Person of Jesus Christ, our Advocate against the accusation of Satan; in the Person of the Father, who loves and forgives us unconditionally, and picks us up when we stumble.

God doesn't just leave us with the mess we've made through our sin, saying, "You got yourself into this. You can just get yourself out of it."

No, He loves us, accepts us, picks us up, brushes us off, and sends us back into the Christian life, speaking words of encouragement and strength to us as we go.

I can recall many times in my own life when I've made wrong moral choices and God in His unsearchable grace has guarded me, kept me safe from the consequences I really deserved.

You can probably think of many similar instances in your own life. In a much greater sense, the good news that Jesus Christ brings us is that God in His grace has intervened so that we don't have to suffer what we deserve to suffer: the *ultimate* consequence of sin, eternal separation from God, that which the Bible calls hell. Jesus paid the eternal price of our sin on the cross.

If you are a follower of Jesus Christ, living a life of repentance toward God, then He is not angry with you anymore. Your sins are forgiven, forgotten, buried in the deepest sea. You have nothing to fear from your heavenly Father.

What Are You Afraid Of?

Perhaps you have made some tragic choices in your life. You may be waiting for the "scales of justice" to be balanced, for the consequences of your sin to be dealt out to you—with interest. You may imagine that God is just biding His time, waiting for the right moment to really hurt you, to knock you down, to finish you off.

Where do you think your fear of God comes from? It certainly doesn't come from the Bible, God's love letter to you and me. God has given you His promise that you have *nothing* to fear from Him.

"You did not receive a spirit that makes you a slave again to fear," says Romans 8:15, "but you received the Spirit of sonship. And by him we cry, 'Abba, Father.' "

Abba is an Aramaic term like "Papa" or "Daddy" in English. In this passage the apostle Paul is telling us that we have a loving, heavenly "Daddy" who wants to heal us, not hurt us. He doesn't wield a whip of fear over us as if we were slaves; He caresses us, His little children, with His fatherly touch of love and forgiveness.

The apostle John tells us, "There is no fear in love. But perfect love drives out fear, because fear has to do with punishment. The man who fears is not made perfect in love."[33]

Do you see the principle in this verse? We fear God because we expect punishment for our sin. But as the experience and knowledge and reality of God's love is perfected in us, our fear will evaporate.

In their book *Guilt and Freedom*, Bruce Narramore and Bill Counts illuminate the psychological dimension of our fear of God and His punishment:

> It's one thing to know that Jesus has paid the penalty
> for our sins, and it's quite another to feel totally free from

punishment. As children, most of us were punished for misdeeds. Our parents weren't able to say, "We are going to punish you one time, and it will take care of all your past, present, and future disobedience." Even if they could have done this, we wouldn't have wanted all that punishment at one time! As a result, we were punished each time we misbehaved. When we became adults we continued to expect punishment. If misdeeds accumulate and no punishment comes, our suspicion grows. We become afraid that when punishment finally arrives, we're *really* going to get it. This causes us to be afraid of God.[34]

From my experience in trying to help people overcome guilt, fear, and self-hate, I really believe that this is the crux of the problem for many individuals. As your guilt grows, multiplies, and compounds, so does your fear of God and His punishment.

But as you come to a more perfect understanding of God's all-consuming love for you, and as you begin to perfect your expression of Christlike unconditional love toward other people, that love will drive out the fear, the misapprehension, the dread of punishment that enslaves you.

We've seen that fear of God has a psychological source. But I believe this fear also has a powerful *spiritual* source. I believe it is instigated, nurtured, and exploited by Satan. Satan is an accuser, a liar, and the father of lies. He wants to immobilize you with fear of punishment, and drive a destructive wedge into the relationship between you and your heavenly Father.

Who will you listen to—the father of lies, or the Father of love and compassion and forgiveness? Romans 16:20 promises, "The God of peace will soon crush Satan under your feet." So throw off the chains of fear that Satan tries to wrap around your mind. Trust God, who has given His Son for you and forgiven all your sins. Spring into loving, forgiving action toward those around you.

God wants to heal us, make us whole, and bring us into a beautiful, joyful, reconciled relationship with Himself. He forgives us freely and completely. We have nothing to fear from God the Father, our "Abba," our heavenly "Daddy."

Consequences Transformed

Perhaps the tragic choices in your life have created some painful circumstances in your life—an unwanted pregnancy, the dissolution of your marriage, the loss of your job or career, the alienation of a friend or family member, public censure, shame, or imprisonment. You may think your life is over or that your usefulness for God is ended.

I want you to know that God's grace is greater than all the sins you have ever committed. No one who turns to God will ever be turned away. God is able to take any circumstances in our lives—including the consequences of our own wrong choices and sins—and transform them into growth and maturity for us and glory for Himself.

As special counsel to President Nixon, Charles Colson was one of the most powerful and respected men in the nation. But the Watergate scandal brought him down from power, shattered his reputation, and caused him to be tried, convicted, and sentenced to prison. Colson made wrong choices, and he suffered the logical consequences of those choices.

But God was able to use those tragic consequences in Colson's life for His own glory, and for the benefit of many people, including Colson himself. He came to know the humbling experience of being publicly disgraced, of being vilified in the press, of being shunned by friends and associates, of having his freedom taken away by due process of law. Stripped of his position and his pride, Colson was starkly confronted with his need of Jesus Christ. With the support and prayers of many Christians, Colson responded and committed himself to the Lord.

Today Chuck Colson is a leading spokesman for Christ in the media, on the public speaking circuit, and through such books as *Born Again* and *Loving God*. Having spent time in prison, he knows something of the special needs of prison inmates, and he has a special ministry of going into prisons and sharing Christ on the inside, while on the outside working vigorously for prison reform.

God wants to take the consequences of your sins and transform them into glory for Himself, growth for your own life, and ministry toward others. He did that kind of miracle in the life of Chuck Colson, and He wants to do a miracle of transformation in your life too. In your life and mine, there are consequences of past sins—some small consequences, others perhaps very great—that we will never be able to change.

We will have to allow God to *use* those consequences to *change us*, to make us more like Him: more loving, more forgiving, more patient, more holy, more selfless. We will have to let God transform the results of our wrongs into His good and His righteousness.

You Can't Afford the Price

Many people know that the Bible promises that God accepts and forgives anyone who comes to Him, that there is no one whose sin is too great for Him to forgive, yet they still find themselves unable to *sense* and *trust* God's forgiving love for them. They tell me, "I go to church and sing, 'The vilest offender who truly believes / That moment from Jesus a pardon receives,' but I just don't *feel* forgiven!"

I believe the reason so many Christians don't feel forgiven is this: We *talk* about being saved by grace through faith, and yet in the back of our minds we are still trying to *earn* God's approval. We haven't really appropriated the free gift of God's forgiveness.

It's as if He is urging us, "Here is salvation. Here is pardon for every sin you ever committed. Take it, it's all yours, no charge."

But in the back of our minds we're thinking, "Okay, I'll take it...but what's the catch? No one could forgive me just like that! Surely I must have to *earn* this somehow!"

We think we have to pay for our sins, *but we know we can't*

afford the price! And thus we miss the peace of knowing that we
are forgiven, cleansed of all unrighteousness.

The author of that great old hymn ''Rock of Ages'' expressed
the truth of our condition well:

> Not the labors of my hands
> Can fulfill Thy law's demands;
> Could my zeal no respite know,
> Could my tears forever flow,
> All for sin could not atone;
> Thou must save, and Thou alone.
>
> Nothing in my hand I bring,
> Simply to Thy cross I cling;
> Naked, come to Thee for dress,
> Helpless, look to Thee for grace;
> Foul, I to the fountain fly,
> Wash me, Savior, or I die!

You can't earn God's approval. Stop trying. Accept His grace,
His forgiveness, His unconditional love. Go to Him empty-
handed—just as you are, without a shred of pride to hide
behind—and simply pour out your need to Him. No matter what
you've done, no matter how great a burden of sin and guilt and
defeat you are carrying, God loves you unconditionally. He accepts you and stands ready to reconcile you to Himself. He wants
to *transform* the consequences of your sins into something beautiful
for your growth, for His glory, and for ministry to other people.

He is your Father. You have nothing to fear.

6

The Fellowship of the Forgiven

In his challenging and encouraging book *Love, Acceptance and Forgiveness*, Jerry Cook tells of an angry phone call he received from the pastor of another church nearby, "a brother I liked and respected then, and still do." This pastor was upset because some of the members of his own church were leaving to go to the church where Jerry Cook pastored. Cook knew that this man needed to get it off his chest, so he let him speak his mind.

In the course of their conversation, this pastor hinted that the people who were moving from his church to Cook's church were only those who were so broken, so beaten down by life or by their sins or by some personal tragedy such as divorce or alcohol abuse that they couldn't really contribute much to the life of a church anyway.

"You know what you are out there?" he finally asked of Jerry Cook. "You're nothing but a bunch of garbage collectors."

Cook mentioned this conversation in church one Sunday, and a man came up to him after the service. He was the man who owned the local garbage collection company, and his face was positively glowing.

"Let me tell you something about garbage," he said. "There's a landfill near here. For ten years we used it as a place to dump trash and garbage. Know what's there now? A beautiful park."

Cook concludes, "I've seen human garbage become beautiful too. I've seen the stench of sin turned into the fragrance of heaven. That's our business. We can't worry about what critics think or say. Where is God going to send the 'garbage' for recycling if He can't put it on our doorstep?"[35]

People need to know that the church is one place where they will be *loved* unconditionally, *accepted* totally and without reservation, and *forgiven* immediately and completely, no matter how terrible their sin, no matter how deep their failure. I believe, based on the Bible, that this is God's vision for every fellowship of believers. "Let us *love* one another."[36] "Accept one another, then, just as Christ accepted you."[37] "Forgive as the Lord forgave you."[38]

Are you and I living out these biblical admonitions today? Are you and I "garbage collectors," welcoming, loving, accepting, and forgiving those who are broken and dying and sick with the stench of sin and failure about them? Are we healing and transforming their unloveliness into the beauty and fragrance of heaven?

Or do we say to those who come to us begging for just a scrap of love, just a crumb of forgiveness, "Go away! You're an embarrassment to us! There's no place here for people like you!" The words of Henry Drummond come back to haunt me again and again: "How many prodigals are kept out of the Kingdom of God by the unlovely characteristics of those who profess to be on the inside?"

According to the Scriptures, we in the church, the body of Jesus Christ, are the fellowship of the forgiven! God calls us to receive His free-flowing forgiveness, and to turn around and pour that same forgiveness out on everyone around us—liberally, lavishly, exuberantly—in gratitude to God for the abundant, extravagant, unconditional love and forgiveness He has given us!

A Community of Healing

A little boy passed a pet store every day on his way home from school. Every day he would stop at that pet store and play with the dozen or so puppies that were kept in a pen in the display window. Finally he got up enough courage to ask the owner of the pet shop how much one of the puppies would cost. The owner of the shop told him the price, and the boy went home and began saving his weekly allowance.

He returned a few weeks later with his piggy bank tucked under his arm. Smiling broadly, he lifted his bank onto the counter and broke it open. "It's all there!" he said joyfully.

"So I see!" said the owner, as he began to sort through the nickels, dimes, and quarters on his counter. "There's the pen. Pick out any puppy you like."

The puppies were yelping, wagging their tails, and crawling all over each other—all but one who sat forlornly in one corner of the pen. The boy reached past all the other puppies, picking up the one lonely puppy in the corner. He brought it to the counter and presented it to the shop owner.

"Oh, you don't want that one," said the man.

"Why not?" asked the boy.

"Well, he's crippled. Just look at his leg. Son, you want a puppy who can run and play with you in the park. You don't want a crippled puppy."

The little boy set the puppy down on the floor and lifted the cuffs of his pants, revealing a set of braces, reminders of a crippling childhood disease of a few years before. "Yes, he's crippled. But I'm crippled too. I thought since we're both crippled, we could be better friends."

We're all crippled, aren't we?

Our wounds come in many different forms, but we're all crippled. We came to Christ to be healed, and in one bold, all-consuming stroke at the cross of Calvary we were healed of the crippling, terminal disease called *sin*. "By His wounds we are healed," says Isaiah 53:5.

But even though we have been healed of the curse of sin, all of us have areas in our lives that are still broken, blighted, painful, or bruised.

Some of us have painful memories that need to be covered by God's grace. Some of us have broken relationships, and we desperately need God's healing touch in our spirit, or in the spirit of that loved one who has bitterly withdrawn himself or herself from us.

Some of us have a bruised or blighted sense of self-esteem, and we need to have God pick us up and say, "You are valuable, My child. You are precious to Me. I created you in My image, and I gave My Son to die for you. That's how greatly I treasure you."

We need God's healing touch. That is why He has placed us in the church. His plan is for the church to be a healing community for all of us broken, crippled, bruised, and bleeding people. But His plan for the church can *only* be carried out as we choose to make our church, our own fellowship of faith, a place where people are loved and accepted and forgiven.

They must be *loved* without conditions—even if their personality doesn't agree with ours; even if their philosophy doesn't agree with ours; even if their political views don't agree with ours; even if their lifestyle doesn't agree with ours.

They must be *accepted* totally, without criticism or prejudice or judgment—even if their behavior doesn't always conform to our standards; even if they don't always dress as we expect people in church to dress; even if they don't easily fit our labels and categories; even if they don't agree with us on major social issues.

They must be *forgiven*—no matter how grievous the sin or how wretched the failure. We must forgive freely, overwhelmingly, unstintingly as we remember God's gracious and complete and lavish forgiveness toward us.

Unless we can do these things, the church *cannot* be a healing community. The church *cannot* touch lives and make broken people whole unless it throws its doors totally, widely open, throws out a broad welcome mat, and proclaims for the world to hear, "Crippled, wounded people are welcome here! We have a place for you. We're in the healing business here, not the judgment business. Come as you are! We'll love you, accept you, and forgive you, no conditions asked, just as God has loved and accepted and forgiven us."

But if we force people to fit into a mold of our making, if we marginally accept them on a tentative kind of probation, if we draw imaginary lines between "our" kind of people and the "wrong" kind of people, then few will ever find God's healing in our church.

A friend of mine, who happens to attend another church, called me recently. He is very crippled in spirit, very broken emotionally. He has found himself caught in a growing web of sin, and he is finding it very hard to extricate himself from that sin. He called me rather than someone in his own church because he was finding no love, no acceptance, no forgiveness in his own church.

"Ron," he said, "I know that what I'm involved in is sin. Part of me recoils in revulsion from this sin in my life, while another part craves it intensely. I'm a walking civil war. But one thing I know: I can talk to you about it, and even though you don't condone what I'm doing, even though you challenge me in a tough and uncompromising way to put this sin completely out of my life, I *know* that you love me and accept me as a brother, right where I am."

I believe this man will find *no healing* in his life until those in his own church, in his own family of faith, accept him and love him too.

Not long ago I was visiting with a young Christian who is struggling to overcome his tendencies toward homosexuality. Since his conversion to Christ, he has become increasingly convicted about his need to deal conclusively with the issue of sexual preferences and practices that have been part of his life for years and years. He has sought prayer and counsel and encouragement for his efforts to remake his style of life into one that is pleasing to God.

But the response of some of the Christians whose understanding and support he has sought has brought tears to his eyes.

"I never thought it would be so hard to find people who would just accept who I am, and pray for me and encourage me where I am," he told me. "Wherever I go, Christians seem to be telling me, '*You change*, and then we'll be able to love you.' I need to find a church home where people will love me *now*, and help me through my struggle."

I believe my young friend will never find healing until he finds a fellowship that will unconditionally love, accept, and forgive him.

Bruce Larson has called the neighborhood bar "possibly the best counterfeit there is to the fellowship Christ wants to give His church. It's an imitation—dispensing liquor instead of grace, escape rather than reality."

Why do people go to a neighborhood bar seeking what the church is supposed to offer? Jerry Cook suggests this answer:

> They're looking for someone who will listen to them. So they get drunk and blow all their problems out on the bartender. He cries along with them and laughs along with them. Then he says, "Okay, it's two o'clock, go on home." So they stagger out and are back the next night for the same thing. What are they looking for? They're looking for love and acceptance. But they can't come to the church because the church doesn't like drunks.[39]

I'm certainly not recommending that churches begin to conduct themselves in the manner of neighborhood taverns, except in this *one* respect: their unconditional *acceptance* of people.

What is the message we send to the hurting, needy people

around us? Is it: "Come on in! There's a place for you here!" Or: "We're all nice *Christians* here: no lonely people, no crippled people, no defeated people, no worn out people, no burned-out people allowed!"

The church *must* be a place where we can put our arms around each other, where we can tell each other, "You're still okay. You're still loved. You're still accepted." That's God's vision for His church. It must be yours and mine too.

Son of Encouragement

There's one person described in the New Testament whose life, more than that of any other Bible character, suggests to me what the church is supposed to be as a community of love and forgiveness. His was a relatively modest and unassuming life; his story doesn't leap out of the pages of Scripture like the life of Paul or Moses. Rather, his story is woven into the fabric of the New Testament—a quiet but penetrating portrait of a man who is unknown to many Christians, but who lived one of the most exemplary lives found in the Word of God.

This man put his arms around other Christians; he affirmed and encouraged them and said, "You're still okay. You're still loved. You're still accepted." Aside from Jesus Christ Himself, this man is unquestionably my favorite New Testament character. His name: *Barnabas*.

The name *Barnabas* is taken from the Hebrew words *bar*, meaning "son," and *nabas*, meaning "encouragement." Barnabas, Son of Encouragement.

The name was given him by the apostles after he came to Christ—a sort of nickname, no doubt, given him to fit his temperament, his personality, his lifestyle, his ministry. Everywhere in the New Testament that you see Barnabas, you see encouragement taking place. He was a man who affirmed others, who unconditionally loved and accepted others, who lovingly exhorted others to a deeper commitment to Jesus Christ.

When Saul—that brutal, murderous persecutor of the

church—was suddenly converted by an encounter with the risen Christ on the road to Damascus, and when all the apostles were afraid of him, thinking his conversion part of a trap, who was there to believe in Saul and disciple him?

Only one man: Barnabas. He embraced Saul, took him around to the apostles, and said, "This man Saul is my brother and yours! Receive him!"

And because Barnabas had the courage to reach out and accept his newfound brother Saul, this onetime persecutor of Christians became the *apostle Paul*, the greatest missionary of all time, and the writer of almost half the books of the New Testament.

When many people, both Jews and Gentiles, were being saved, were coming together in one big fellowship in Antioch, the apostles in Jerusalem knew the tensions and deep cultural clashes that were bound to occur there. So who could they send to heal those divisions and ease those tensions? Who else but the Son of Encouragement, Barnabas?

So Barnabas went to Antioch, and "encouraged them all to remain true to the Lord with all their hearts. He was a good man, full of the Holy Spirit and faith, and a great number of people were brought to the Lord."[40] That's the kind of man he was.

According to 2 Corinthians 1:3,4, the call to love and encourage one another, to be a Barnabas to one another, is upon every Christian. God encourages and comforts and accepts us in our trials, in our brokenness, so that we in turn can lavish that same ministry of encouragement on others around us.

The ministry of encouragement is commanded of every believer, without exception: "Encourage one another and build each other up."[41]

Tony Campolo writes, "God has called you to be what Barnabas was—a son or daughter of encouragement, a person who creates in others the ability for them to believe in themselves. God wants you to be the kind of person who makes everybody that you meet feel gloriously wonderful, self-assured, and precious."[42]

That's the ministry of encouragement, as God is teaching us through the person of Barnabas. It's a ministry He intends for every member of the body of Christ.

Who has been a Barnabas to you? Have you been a Barnabas, an encourager, to anyone lately?

Perhaps you don't know where to begin. Perhaps you don't know how to go about being an encourager to someone else. Let me give you four pointers that can get you started.

1. *Affirm, don't flatter.*

If you're going to authentically *encourage* people, then you need to learn to *affirm* them—not just flatter them or show appreciation for something they've done or the way they look or the way they behave. To truly affirm another person, you need to unconditionally attest to his *worth as a person*, not his achievements or his appearance. Certainly it's good to appreciate what a person does, but it's *essential* to affirm *who a person is!* Appreciation comes and goes, depending on achievements or failures; unconditional affirmation is *always* there.

2. *Be specific.*

Examples: "I really see the hand of God on your life in a unique and special way, because you have a boldness that is so rare in the church today." Or, "I've watched the way you relate to people, and I just want you to know that I believe in you, and in the fact that God can use your gentleness and sensitivity to heal and comfort others."

All of us need to learn how to find *specific* ways to encourage our fellow Christians, our marriage partners, and our children— especially our children! In my own home, I sit down with my two children at bedtime, and we pray together. In those moments I try to find specific ways to affirm and encourage my children, to let them know I'm on their side, that I believe in them.

"Rachael," I often say to my nine-year-old, "I notice you have a book there. You really love to read, don't you? You're going to get to read even better and better. Maybe someday you'll even want to write some books that other people will read."

Or, "You know, Rachael, God has made you slender and

tall and able to run fast. It was fun the other day to watch you at the track meet, and I just hope that as you grow older, and stronger, and faster, you'll run for Jesus.''

"Nathan," I often say to my six-year-old, "you're the kind of guy who brings a lot of happiness into my life, and into a lot of lives. That's just the way God made you. Nathan, you're the biggest kid in your class, and it makes me feel good to hear what your teacher told me the other day, that you try to protect some of the smaller kids from the bully in the class. That shows courage, and that shows love for those other kids, and I know that makes Jesus happy."

I'm trying to be a Barnabas to my kids.

If we are not *specific and genuine* as we affirm our children, our marriage partners, our friends, our brothers and sisters in Christ, then our attempts to authentically affirm others will be transformed into little more than trite flattery.

3. *Affirm spiritual gifts.*

One of the key ways we discover our spiritual gifts is when other people in the church discern those gifts in us, then have the courage to come to us and specifically affirm those gifts in us, face-to-face. This is one of the most important responsibilities that we have toward our brothers and sisters in Christ.

First we need to study the various passages of Scripture that describe spiritual gifts: Romans 12:4-8; 1 Corinthians 12; Ephesians 4:11-16; and 1 Peter 4:9-11. Then we need to say to our Christian brother or sister, "I see in you the gift of showing mercy, or hospitality, or teaching, or evangelism. I want to encourage you in that, and to pray that God will continue to develop and exercise that gift in you, and to release that spiritual gift for ministry in our church. I want to help you be the best you can be for Jesus Christ."

I know from firsthand experience the importance of this ministry of affirming spiritual gifts in other people. There was a period of time, shortly after I gave my life to Christ, when I was very unsure of what God had in store for me, and I had an abysmally low self-image. And if a few people hadn't had the courage to take the initiative right then, and come to me and affirm the gifts they saw in me, I would never have developed any of the gifts that God has since allowed me to use.

4. *Accept others unconditionally.*

As Christians, while we might not always accept the *behavior* of other people, we are responsible as followers of Jesus Christ to always accept people where they are, and to love them unconditionally. One of the most disillusioning things to me as a Christian is to see how often we as Christians not only reject the wrong behavior of a brother who is taken in some fault, but we reject the *brother* as well!

When we accept others, we allow them to be uniquely who they are. They don't have to meet our standards or preconditions in order to be fully one with us in the body of Christ. They can talk honestly about their feelings, about their ideas, about their hopes, about their doubts—and it doesn't change a thing. When we accept others, they feel safe, they feel whole, they feel released from anyone's judgment.

We can disagree with each other. We can even correct each other when the occasion requires it (as we are admonished to in Galatians 6:1). But no one will ever think less of anyone, or reject anyone, or exclude anyone, or avoid anyone because of who they are, or what they say, or what they think or do. Love and acceptance cover multitudes of sins, differences, and disagreements.

Wouldn't it be something if unconditional love so marked your life that those people around you who fail, who are beaten down by their sin, who have been broken by tragedy or scandal or a bruised self-image, could know that there is *one* person they can go to and find total acceptance, extravagant forgiveness, and potent encouragement?

Wouldn't it be something if your church was so marked by mutual encouragement and love that when the people in your community mentioned your church, they would say, "That church? Oh, that's the Barnabas Bunch! They're just a bunch of Barnabases over there, always encouraging and accepting and loving each other so much!''

Wouldn't it be something?

A Community of Unity

I know that of the many people who read these words, many different varieties of experience are represented, many different levels of commitment to Christ and His church.

You may be intensely active in your church—an elder, or a deacon, or a Sunday school teacher. You may be actively involved in helping, in serving, in working with the missions work or the evangelism work or the property care work. You may be involved in a small, close-knit fellowship of believers, such as a home Bible study or a house church. If so, I commend you for that, and encourage you to keep on, and to keep building those qualities of loving, accepting, forgiving, and encouraging others into your life as you relate to your brothers and sisters in close Christian fellowship.

It may be, however, that you have not actively involved yourself in the life of a local body of believers. You may believe that it's enough to have a relationship with God. You may think a close relationship with other Christians is optional: ''It's okay for those who really need it, but I don't need anyone else; I have Jesus.''

You may attend church every Sunday, slipping into the back of the church at the beginning of the service, then slipping out again during the last hymn so you don't have to greet anyone or shake anyone's hand. Or you may just attend on Christmas and Easter.

Perhaps you used to be very actively involved in the church, but someone hurt you, wounded you with an unkind word or a cruel act, many years ago. You want to keep your relationship with God, but you never want to get close enough to other people in the church to let them hurt you like that again.

So you have withdrawn, pulled away from the church. Your contact with God is through your prayers, through reading the

Bible, through Christian books like the one you are reading right now, or through televised church services.

If you have distanced yourself from the body of Christ, if you feel that you can be what God wants you to be apart from being joined to a local fellowship of believers, then you have not understood what the Bible teaches about God's plan for your life. Christians are called to be a community together—a fellowship of the forgiven, a community of unity, a family of unconditional love.

Over the years I have met many scores of Christians who sincerely love Jesus Christ, but who have no deep commitment to living in intense, vulnerable community with their brothers and sisters in Jesus Christ. Instead, they strive to live in their own self-sufficiency, championing the American philosophy of rugged individualism.

Tragically, they are living a lifestyle of total denial of what the Bible teaches about the nature of the church and the nature of the Christian.

According to the Bible, there are two crucial reasons why each of us, as individual followers of Christ, must strive for community and unity in fellowship with other believers: 1) God is glorified when we are unified; and 2) Jesus Christ is demonstrated to be alive in the world when we are unified.

In John 17, the beautiful high-priestly prayer of our Lord just before He went to the cross, He offers to God the Father three essential petitions: 1) that God the Father and God the Son would be glorified; 2) that His followers—including later generations of followers, you and I—would be unified, as Jesus and His Father are one; and 3) that the world would come to know Jesus through the unity and love of His followers.

Jesus ties our unity to God's glory and the world's coming to know Jesus Christ. Accordingly, if you are in a broken relationship with another Christian, or if you are holding back from becoming committed to a local body of believers, then you are making a serious and tragic choice: You are deciding that in this area of your life you consciously refuse to give glory to God!

In our unity we bear witness to the fact that the resurrection has taken place in our lives, that Jesus Christ is alive in the world!

Through His church around the world, Jesus is establishing a new and unified society in the midst of a fragmented society.

Through His church, Jesus is establishing a new and unified family in the midst of so many broken and fragmented families.

Through His church, Jesus is establishing an alternative community in the midst of strife-torn, hate-filled, dying communities.

Through His church, Jesus is establishing a unified fellowship of the forgiven in the midst of an unforgiving world. The basis of that new society, that new family, that new community, is *unity* rooted in unconditional love.

The key question that now confronts us is this: Are we interested in being faithful to the truth that God has revealed to us about His church? Are we vitally concerned about making Him visible in the world by living out His life in our own lives, in our relationships with one another? Are we committed to becoming a fellowship of the forgiven, a community of unity, projecting Christ's image before the world through the lens of our common, integrated life together?

The late Dr. Francis Schaeffer was profoundly right when he said, "The Church today needs not only an orthodoxy of doctrine. It needs an orthodoxy of community."

We need to match our orthodoxy of belief with an orthodoxy of unity, an orthodoxy of unconditional love that will outcare and outdare the unforgiving world in which we live. We need to be winning people to Jesus Christ as much with our lives as with our words.

The church is to be the reflector, the mirror, of the wisdom of God: "His intent was that now, *through the church*, the manifold wisdom of God should be made known."[43] The church is God's chosen means to bring glory to Himself: "To him be glory *in the church*."[44] The church is the object of Christ's love: "*Christ loved the church* and gave himself up for her to make her holy."[45]

The church may be flawed and imperfect, filled as it is with flawed and sinful human beings, but God's view of the church is superlative. He hasn't given up on the church. Have you?

If you are distancing yourself from one other believer, or from the body of Christ, then you are being tragically unfaithful to the biblical doctrine of the church. Until you join the fellowship of the forgiven, committing yourself to producing and preserving the unity of the body of Christ, God will not be able to use you as an instrument of His unconditional love and peace, as a means of proclaiming His glory and forgiveness to an unforgiving world.

The Divided Kingdom

The church is on the attack!

The church is on the offensive!

The church is marching against its enemies!

Sadly, it seems that the people we are spending most of our militant energies on are *other Christians*! The church may be an army, but this "Christian army" in undoubtedly the only army in history that ever attacked its own wounded.

One of our favorite means of attacking each other is by *labels*. We are masters at pigeonholing each other. We have so many labels to separate us "authentic Christians" from those "misguided" or "unbiblical" or "naive" or even "pseudo-Christian" brothers and sisters with whom we disagree.

David Augsburger puts it well in his book *The Freedom of Forgiveness*:

> Labels are not only a sign of mental stagnation in the user, they aren't exactly healthy for the person labeled either.
>
> To begin with, they're seldom true. Labels are libels. In print, there's only a one-letter difference between *label* and *libel*. In speech, there's usually less. It may be just a wrinkled nose or a raised eyebrow. All it takes to paste someone with a label is an ordinary word smeared with just the right inflection of the voice, contortion of the

face or distortion of the truth. . . .[46]

Many of us in the church have grown so weary of all the name-calling, the labeling, the libeling, the infighting of Christian against Christian that we became burned-out, worn-out, and cast-out before we even got a chance to take on the real enemy—the principalities and powers of this unforgiving world. We've forgotten that Jesus didn't come to take sides; He came to *take over*, to set up His kingdom. How can He do that as long as His kingdom is divided against itself?

In Mark 9:38-40 John came to Jesus and said, "Teacher, we saw a man driving out demons in your name and we told him to stop, because he was not one of us."

How many of us grumble about other ministries, other denominations, other churches, other Christians, and would like to be able to tell them, "Stop what you're doing!" because they're not "one of us"?

But notice Jesus' surprising reply: "Do not stop him. No one who does a miracle in my name can in the next moment say anything bad about me, for whoever is not against us is for us."

Unity in Diversity

There's no room in the church for *division*, but there is unlimited room in the church for *diversity*. We need to remember this when we are tempted to close our hearts to other believers because they have a different philosophy of ministry, a different style of worship, a different set of spiritual gifts, a different temperament, a different mode of baptism, a different doctrine on some marginal issue, or a different vocabulary and way of expressing their faith.

Notice the attitude of Paul: "Some preach Christ out of envy and rivalry, but others out of good will. The latter do so in love, knowing that I am put here for the defense of the gospel. The former preach Christ out of selfish ambition, not sincerely, supposing that they can stir up trouble for me while I am in chains.

But what does it matter? The important thing is that in every way, whether from false motives or true, Christ is preached. And because of this I rejoice.''[47]

How about you? Do you rejoice to hear that people are coming to Christ, even if they do so in churches with which you disagree over some secondary doctrine or issue?

Do you rejoice to see a prominent professing Christian giving his testimony on national television, even if he represents a different political persuasion than yours?

Do you rejoice that Christ is preached, no matter what the means, no matter what the motives, no matter who the preacher?

If Paul can rejoice that someone preaches Christ with the sole motive of causing personal trouble for him, then certainly you and I can rejoice whenever the gospel goes out, no matter who is the preacher, no matter what the motive, no matter what he espouses as a side issue or political persuasion.

Regardless of what distinguishes us from one another, we can *always* unite with other brothers and sisters around the one Center that is common to us all: the Person of Jesus Christ. Such unconditional acceptance of other Christians with differing views is all too rare, according to my experience.

But I know it's possible: I've seen it happen. And what's more, it's God's unconditional *command* to the church: ''Accept one another, then, just as Christ accepted you, in order to bring praise to God.''[48]

God has given us the freedom to be diverse, to exhibit many facets, to display a rainbow-colored faith to the world so that we in His church can become ''all things to all men so that by all possible means''[49] we might project Christ to people of different temperaments, persuasions, lifestyles, and cultures. Moreover, God *commands* that we have total unity in our splendid diversity.

We are *one* fellowship, the fellowship of the forgiven.

Let us *love* each other unconditionally, as Christ has loved us.

Let us *accept* each other, embracing each other in an exalted community of unity, which brings glory to God.

Let us *encourage* each other, affirming each other and exhorting each other to even deeper commitment to the kingdom of God.

And let us *forgive* each other, as God in Christ has forgiven us.

Christians in Conflict

7

The headline of the newspaper article read: "Two Factions—One Fellowship?" The story that followed was the true account of a church that was seeking to find a pastor. The church was polarized. There were two different factions, both of them contentious, strong-willed, and determined to get their own favorite man to come and serve as the new pastor. The news article read something like this:

> Yesterday each faction sent its choice for minister to the same pulpit. Both spoke simultaneously, each trying to shout the other down. Both called for hymns, and the congregation sang two different songs at the same time, each side attempting to drown the other out.
>
> Before the hymns were concluded, both groups began shouting at each other. Bibles were raised in anger. The

> Sunday morning service dissolved into chaos as both preachers continued to outshout each other with their sermons.
>
> Finally one of the deacons called the police. A few minutes later two police officers came in and ordered the congregation—or congregations—to be quiet and return to their homes. The rivals filed out, still arguing.
>
> That evening one of the members of the church called a "Let's Be Friends" meeting. It ended in a brawl.

Our conflicts are not always as public or as ludicrous as this one, which was splashed across the pages of many newspapers. But the world is watching as the church fights its civil wars. The world shakes its head in amazement as Christians are wounded and crushed and devoured by other Christians. The gospel of love and forgiveness is brought down in shame and discredit as the world sees unforgiving Christians battle each other in unforgiving churches.

In Russia in 1917 the Bolshevik party was boldly, efficiently, ruthlessly carrying out its plans for revolution, overturning the oppressive government of the czars and putting in place another oppressive government, a government characterized by the atheistic philosophy called Communism.

At the very same time, on the very same day, the largest Christian denomination in Russia was holding an all-day meeting. The meeting was filled with harsh, vindictive conflict, all centered on one divisive issue. What was the issue? Was it how the Christian church should respond to the new government that was coming into power? Was it how the church would carry out its mission under the oppression of avowedly atheist rule?

No, the issue was the *candles* in the sanctuaries of the Russian churches! The church was bitterly divided over whether they should be 18 inches or 22 inches high!

Conflict Just Is

Conflict is a part of life. It exists in marriage. It exists in parent-child relationships. It exists between employers and employees.

It exists between neighbors. It exists between fellow Christians in the church throughout the world. It has always been and will always be.

I agree with David Augsburger: "Conflict isn't necessarily good or bad, right or wrong. Conflict just *is*. How we view, approach, and work through our differences does to a large extent determine our whole life pattern."

Conflict is inevitable in life. Yet it is always within our power to control our *response* to conflict. Conflict can either destroy us and rip apart our relationships, or else conflict can be used to bring about change and growth, to strengthen relationships, to spur innovation and new ways of looking at our tasks. The difference between the kind of conflict that destroys and that which brings growth is found in the human will, your will and mine. The choice is ours.

Philipp Melanchthon (1497-1560), the great reformer and co-worker with Martin Luther, coined a motto that I believe expresses very well what our response as Christians should be when conflict arises:

> In the essentials, unity.
> In nonessentials, liberty.
> In all things, charity.

Put another way, "Unity in the essentials, tolerance in the nonessentials, love in all things."

In our homes, our churches, and our offices we are surrounded by tensions. Often these are *creative* tensions between two philosophical approaches, two stylistic approaches, or two sets of honestly held convictions. This is an entirely good and growth-inducing thing to happen, as long as we keep a right, loving, accepting spirit toward each other.

However, if our philosophy, style, opinions, or ambitions begin to take precedence over our love and acceptance of each other, then our *creative* tensions will flare into *destructive* emotions that will brutally dismember our relationships.

Legalists in the Church

These kinds of tensions are nothing new or unique to the twentieth century. We readily find such tensions and conflicts as we examine the history of the early church in the New Testament. For example, Acts 15 tells about a time when Christians were in conflict, arguing over exactly what were the *essentials* that new Gentile believers needed to observe in the Christian faith.

The passage records that there were Jewish Christians—specifically those Christians "who belonged to the party of the Pharisees"—who were teaching new Gentile converts that it was *essential* that they be circumcised according to Old Testament law in order to be saved. Paul, however, believed circumcision to be a *nonessential,* an option, a matter of Christian freedom and tolerance. What was at stake in Paul's mind was whether Christianity would become a faith for all people everywhere, or whether it would become little more than a new branch of Judaism, open only to those who followed the Hebrew traditions.

Paul wisely realized that the big issues in life do not just solve themselves, that conflict had to be confronted head-on. So he courageously waded into the difficult controversy, taking the issue before the Council of Elders at Jerusalem. There, as Acts 15:5 records, "Some of the believers who belonged to the party of the Pharisees stood up and said, 'The Gentiles *must* be circumcised and *required* to obey the law of Moses.' "

Rigid, harsh, unyielding, dogmatic words! These Pharisee believers left *no room* for compromise or even dialogue. Our conflicts in the church today are often fought in the same heated, uncompromising terms. The issues aren't Jew-Gentile tensions anymore, but the divisions are just as deep. We have multiple factions within one fellowship. We have "our kind of people" versus "the wrong kind of people," "us" versus "them," and we write each other off as naive, as uncommitted, as inauthentic—because "they don't do things *our* way."

We may be tempted to view these harsh legalists in Acts 15:5 as false teachers, outsiders who had come into the Church to stir up trouble. But no, they are clearly called "believers"—

Pharisee Christians. They were harsh, they were confrontive, they were on the wrong side of the issue—but they were *authentic believers*. Remember that whenever you're tempted to dismiss someone you disagree with in your church.

There were Pharisees in the early Church, and the Pharisee spirit is still with us today. You see, we can never be too smug about "those Pharisees over there." After all, smugness— prideful self-righteousness—was the very sin which caused Jesus to denounce the Pharisees of His day so vehemently. So if you seek to politically outmaneuver and outflank the "opposition" in your church, or if you pride yourself on being part of the "orthodox, biblical, truly Christian" faction of your church, or if you demand that all ministry in your church be done according to your philosophy and vision—then *you* are the Pharisee in your church!

A Wise Compromise

Acts 15:7 tells us that "After there had been much discussion, Peter got us and addressed them." The eloquent speech of Peter, together with the persuasive arguments of Paul and Barnabas, became the basis of a dynamic new ministry toward the Gentile world. The Council reached a wise compromise in which Gentile believers would not be bound by Jewish legalism, but were simply commanded to avoid immorality and ceremonially impure foods. Thus Gentile believers became equal partners with Jewish believers, and the church began to expand in totally new ways.

But this did not happen before there was *much* debate, *much* discussion, and *much* conflict. There was a freedom to express feelings and concerns. And there was an openness, a willingness to change one's mind, and to do *all* of this in love. We are impacted in every generation because of the wise compromise that was reached in Acts 15. Today, because of that very decision, the gospel of love and forgiveness goes out with power into the whole world.

Our paramount concern in all our relationships with each other has to be *unity in love*—not issues, not tasks, not strategies, not philosophies. And at those times when we find ourselves in conflict, and there is no clear-cut violation of a biblical command at stake, then *wise compromise* is a bridge that can bring reconciliation and unity between believers.

Compromise, for the sake of unity in the body of Christ, is not necessarily a sign of weakness. It can be a sign of courage and obedience, a demonstration of the fact that we're strong enough in nonessentials to give and take, so that the *essential* quality of our relationship with each other—our *unity*—can be maintained.

Conflict and Church Leadership

Are you a lay leader in a church—an elder or deacon or board member or Sunday school teacher? Are you a pastor? Then you should know that the Bible gives you special guidance regarding conflict with other Christians. Paul writes, "Don't have anything to do with foolish and stupid arguments, because you know they produce quarrels. And the Lord's servant must not quarrel; instead, he must be kind to everyone, able to teach, not resentful. Those who oppose him he must gently instruct, in the hope that God will grant them repentance leading them to a knowledge of the truth."[50]

It's inevitable that conflicts will come, but so many senseless, foolish quarrels are started by Christians who love to argue for argument's sake. This, says Paul, we must have nothing to do with. Rather, the mature servant of God is called upon to gently—*gently!*—instruct and correct and teach others.

This is good advice for every Christian to build into his life. But it is particularly crucial that Christians in positions of responsibility learn to deal with conflict in gentleness and love. When conflict arises, we should not be quarrelsome, but rather kind and gentle, differing with our brothers and sisters in love.

Sometimes the struggle in times of conflict becomes too much for us to handle alone. At such times we need to seek out Christian counsel. Often our tendency, especially for those of us in positions of leadership, is to view such an option as an admission of weakness. I assure you from my own experience that seeking competent (including professional) Christian counsel to help us through times of conflict is a sign of strength, not weakness. How all of us—and especially us self-reliant, ruggedly individualistic *men*—need to know that!

On two occasions in my adult life I have been involved in conflict that has been so intense, so difficult, so complex in its ramifications that I knew I couldn't handle it alone. So on both of those occasions I sought out professional Christian counsel. I spent many painful but restorative hours, working through my conflict with a competent Christian counselor, a man whose wisdom and deep Christian commitment I could trust. And I came through those times stronger, more resilient, and better equipped to counsel others in their trials and conflicts.

It's not a sign of weakness to seek professional help. No, it's a sign of weakness when we *refuse* to acknowledge our need, *refuse* to deal with our need decisively, and *refuse* to courageously take the necessary measures to become whole and well. God has given us the precious gift of life, and one of the greatest gifts we can give back to Him is our commitment to do whatever is necessary to become whole, complete people in Jesus Christ, no matter how much work and pain is involved in that process.

We prove our maturity and strength not by hiding the conflict within us, not by running from the struggle, but by honestly, openly facing the conflict. When conflict comes, immature people avoid it, while mature people stay and face it and work through the conflict to a point of understanding and reconciliation and wholeness.

You may be facing a conflict right now that is so painful that you are considering the option of running—of leaving your church, of separating from a spouse, of distancing yourself from a fellow Christian. Please know that a sign of maturity in Christ is that you *stay*, that you hang in there and make a difference, knowing that Jesus Christ is with you in the midst of your conflict, ready to administer His healing touch of love.

The Benefits of Conflict

Some conflicts in our lives can be beneficial, bringing growth, renewal, and positive change. Times of conflict can enable you to discover and develop faith and strength of character you never knew you had—*if* you are open to what God is trying to show you through that conflict.

Another benefit of conflict is that it is often *only* in such times that we are forced to honestly evaluate ourselves. I'm slowly learning that when someone approaches me with a concern about my life, my first response should not be to defend myself. Rather, I should ask myself, "Is this concern valid? Is there some truth to this criticism?" I know that in my own life such times of conflict, as painful as they have often been, have contributed to my growth, to my becoming more fully what God wants me to be.

Conflict is never easy. We know that, and thus we tend to put it off, to delay it, to duck it—and the tensions inevitably get worse. And this very human tendency to avoid rather than face and resolve conflict often leads to the most difficult form of conflict of all: an intense *inner* conflict which eats away at us and compounds the tension between ourselves and someone else. In such times we need the grace and strength of God to enable us to meet the challenge of conflict head-on, to resolve it, and to get on with the joyful business of living in peace with one another. When we respond to conflict in a courageous, Christlike way through reliance upon God, He can use that conflict to bring about His good.

A Clash of Temperaments

In her book *Caught in the Conflict*, Leilani Watt, wife of former Reagan White House Cabinet official James Watt, relates the compelling story of how she discovered the grace of God in the midst of being caught in the conflict and controversy surrounding her husband—a conflict which ultimately led to his resignation as Secretary of the Interior. The Watts are committed followers of Jesus Christ, and they've attained more first-hand experience about *conflict* than you and I are ever likely to know.

Early in the book she tells of the inner conflict she faced shortly after her marriage to James, as she began to realize how different in temperament she and her new husband were:

> Within months it became evident that our personality differences were going to cause me acute discomfort.... James was a driver, willing to push forward and make things happen, even if it made other people uncomfortable, whereas I never wanted to upset anyone. I could be supportive of people with totally opposite viewpoints, unwilling to take a stand. James was decisive, never looking back once he had made a decision. I found it hard to make a decision if I felt someone might disapprove. He was sometimes dominating while trying to convince others of his position. I would never push my point of view for fear that other people wouldn't like me.... James was a risk-taker. I wanted to play it safe....
>
> I hated conflict.[51]

The differences she describes between herself and James Watt remind me of the differences between Paul and Barnabas. Paul was a driver, willing to push forward, to make things happen, decisive and strong-willed, opinionated and domineering. Barnabas was an encourager, a man who just wanted to affirm others, to believe in others, to help others believe in themselves. In short, Paul was task-oriented; Barnabas was people-oriented.

Whereas the first half of Acts 15 tells the story of how one conflict was successfully resolved by the Council of Elders in Jerusalem, the latter half of that same chapter tells the sad but instructive story of a conflict that arose between Paul and Barnabas—a conflict which I believe arose out of a clash of temperaments.

The conflict between Paul and Barnabas is over a young man named John Mark. This young man had accompanied Paul and Barnabas as an assistant on their first missionary journey, but

when things got tough—possibly because of persecution or disease
or hardship—John Mark *quit*, deserting Paul and Barnabas at
Pamphylia.[52]

Thus in Acts 15, as Paul and Barnabas prepared for their
second missionary journey, the question between them was
this: "Should John Mark—a quitter, a defector—be given a
second chance?" Barnabas voted *yes*. Paul voted an emphatic
no. And thus these two great men of God became locked in *conflict*.

I can just picture Barnabas pleading from the depth of his great
encourager's heart: "Paul, I believe in John Mark. I really see
growth in him. He deserves a second chance. To reject him now,
while he's so repentant and remorseful, while he's trying to get
his life turned around, would do him so much harm!" Good
old Barnabas: compassionate, people-oriented, always the
encourager.

Yet the hardheaded, task-oriented, decisive, and strong-willed
apostle Paul surely had a strong case as well: "No, Barnabas,
no! John Mark deserted us in Pamphylia, and he forsook the
work of the gospel! Where was he when we needed him, Barnabas? Where was he when we were nearly stoned to death,
Barnabas? We can't rely on him! Our *goal*, our *mission*, our
work is too important for us to take a chance on John Mark
again!"

People-oriented Barnabas was looking at the man, John Mark,
and his emotional and spiritual needs. But task-oriented Paul
was looking at the ministry, at the hard work ahead, at the *task*
of the Great Commission. And the person-oriented temperament
began to clash with the task-oriented temperament. This happens in many of our churches today, but it also happens in our
marriage relationships, in our parent-child relationships, and
in relationships at work or between friends. And the result is
conflict, sometimes *intense* conflict.

Acts 15:39 makes it clear that the conflict between these two
men was so intense that there would be no resolution: "They
had such a sharp disagreement that they parted company." Barnabas took John Mark with him to Cyprus while Paul chose Silas

to go with him to Syria and Cilicia. Two mature, Spirit-led, godly men were now separated because of a clash of temperaments. There was no doctrinal or moral issue at stake here. The Bible does not explicitly commend one decision or the other on this matter. There was validity on both sides.

But rather than compromise and work through their differences to a solution, they separated. There is tragedy in that separation; there is a deep sense of loss and sorrow. What's more, we now see something in Paul and Barnabas that we would rather not see: a spirit of stubborn inflexibility, issuing in a division. Again we see that the Bible never flatters its heroes. Rather, the Word of God demonstrates its integrity as it gives us an honest account of the people we encounter in its pages.

We Need Each Other

What can we learn from the tragic dissolution of this great friendship?

First, we should remember that conflict between two Christians is not necessarily a sign of immaturity: Two committed, Christ-centered, biblically-based Christians will not always agree. You may be in a close, Spirit-filled relationship with Christ, and so may your brother or sister in Christ, and you still may have a major conflict over a given issue or decision.

Second, we should remember that in times of conflict when there is no explicit biblical command involved, *both* sides have validity. As hard as that is for some of us to believe—especially if we're given to a strong-willed, forceful, uncompromising temperament—there will be many conflicts between Christians where no absolute biblical command has been given, and both sides of the issue have several valid points. If the conflict is not wisely resolved through compromise, then *both sides lose.*

Paul and Barnabas lost a great deal when they parted company. Paul lost the companionship of the man who first believed in him, first discipled him. Barnabas lost the companionship of the greatest missionary who ever lived. These two men, who had encouraged and discipled each other for so many years, who had traveled so many torturous miles together for the cause of Christ, threw it all away in one dispute. They *needed* each other, yet they *forsook* each other.

As Barnabas and John Mark set sail for Cyprus, they sailed out of the book of Acts, never to appear again. The book on my favorite New Testament character is now closed.

We don't hear of Barnabas again after his conflict with Paul, but we *do* know that Barnabas was faithful and obedient to God when he forgave and reinstated John Mark against Paul's objections. Barnabas believed in John Mark, even though John Mark could not believe in himself. Barnabas pulled John Mark back into the ministry when he was ready to give up on himself, and eventually John Mark was restored to wholeness and usefulness for God.

Even the great apostle Paul finally had to "eat his words"— and I believe he did so with joy—as he wrote, "Get Mark and bring him with you, because he is helpful to me in my ministry."[53] Paul must have had many occasions to ponder, "Where would John Mark be today if Barnabas hadn't continued believing in him after I gave up on him? And where would I be without this helpful, profitable co-worker, John Mark?"

I've heard so many people use this story of Paul's conflict with Barnabas as an excuse for not seeking reconciliation with a brother or sister in Christ, or with a marriage partner. They glibly say, "Well, Paul and Barnabas couldn't agree on John Mark, and they went their separate ways. So I guess it's okay for me and my friend, my co-worker, or my marriage partner to do the same thing."

Understand that what is recorded in Acts 15 is what *actually happened*, not necessarily what God ideally *wanted* to happen. But what God wants to happen in your life and mine is that we become *agents of reconciliation*! Only when we are unified can we bring glory to God.

If you are contemplating a separation from another Christian or from your husband or wife, then I challenge you to read John 17, Christ's prayer for you before His death on the cross.

Read His prayer that God would be glorified by *our unity* with one another—then say to Him if you can, ''Not so, Lord! I will *not* honor Your will for me! I choose to break this relationship with the full knowledge that in doing so I am breaking Your heart of love. I choose disobedience rather than reconciliation.''

Can you honestly do that? I pity you if you can.

Certainly, there are truths to be discovered in the story of Paul's conflict with Barnabas, but they are truths that are in harmony with the direct commands of Scripture. God does not send us mixed signals in His Word. He doesn't command ''accept one another'' in one place, then suggest ''reject those who disagree with you'' in another.

Paul's Regrets

Paul's conflict with Barnabas came fairly early in his career as an apostle. It may well have been the end of their relationship, or perhaps they later had an opportunity to patch their differences, forgive each other, and love each other. The Scriptures don't tell us. But I believe this sad experience taught Paul many lessons which he later shared with other Christians through his letters.

Maybe Paul was thinking back in remorse over his refusal to accept John Mark in his weakness and to bear with his failings when he wrote, ''We who are strong ought to bear with the failings of the weak.... Accept one another, then, just as Christ accepted you, in order to bring praise to God.''[54]

Perhaps Paul was grieving over his broken relationship with Barnabas when he wrote, ''Bear with each other and forgive whatever grievances you may have against one another. Forgive as the Lord forgave you.''[55]

Certainly Paul came to know that conflict is just a part of life, even between mature, Spirit-filled Christians. But Paul, speaking from tragic experience, wants you to know that in all our conflicts we must exemplify a spirit of love, grace, gentleness, and acceptance—a spirit which always seeks to see the *other* side in a conflict. Our unity, our fellowship with each other, transcends any of the issues over which we may become divided. We must do all we can to preserve that unity.

Sit and Talk or Stand and Fight?

Many people today are ready to give up on the church. I'm not. I have seen so much caring, so much forgiveness, so much genuine reconciliation and healing unconditional love expressed in the body of Christ over the years. So I get a little fed up with the attitude I sometimes hear that the church is no longer effective, that it's too divided to be used by God anymore. No, the Church is still God's means of bringing glory to Himself, spiritual and emotional wholeness to Christians, and the word of salvation to the world. God has not given up on the church, whatever its flaws, and neither should we.

But how tragic the impact that fights and brawls and unforgiveness in times of conflict are having in church after church in America today! How tragic that we unbendingly choose to stand and fight while God pleads with us over and over, throughout His Word, to sit and talk through our differences in a spirit of gentleness and love, to resolve our conflicts with grace and peace!

Certainly there *are* truths "worth fighting for," truths for which we must take a firm (but loving and gentle) stand. We must never compromise the fact that our absolute center is Jesus Christ; that our absolute authority in everything is nothing more or less than the Bible; that our only hope for salvation is grace through faith apart from works.

But while God clearly calls us to take a firm stand on these truths of the Christian faith, He just as clearly calls us to the task of keeping peace, maintaining unity, forgiving in love, and demonstrating unconditional acceptance and grace. Paul writes, "You, my brothers, were called to be free. But do not use your freedom to indulge the sinful nature; rather, serve one another in love. The entire law is summed up in a single command: 'Love your neighbor as yourself.' If you keep on biting and devouring each other, watch out or you will be destroyed by each other."[56]

There are plenty of potential issues for conflict in a church: differences over music, style of worship, the importance of innovation versus preservation of tradition, philosophy of ministry, frequency of communion, scheduling of meetings, the number of church officers, administrative style, personality differences, or Sunday school curriculum. But not one of these is an essential issue which the Bible conclusively addresses. They are simply matters of taste and personal preference. And if the Holy Spirit is not in control of us, we will fight to the end to have our way.

I've seen it happen over and over again. Good, loving, committed Christians have been devoured and destroyed by other Christians. Some have left the ministry, others have left the church. Some have been so wounded and disillusioned that they have even left their faith. How this must break the heart of God!

Conflict is inevitable in life, in the home, in the church—but fights and brawls and division and unforgiveness are always regrettable and avoidable. Even though conflict is hard and sometimes painful, it should always be faced—but our conflicts can always be resolved in love, in a spirit of gentleness, in a spirit of mutual acceptance, affirmation, and peace.

My prayer is that Jesus Christ will mold His church into a family of forgiven brothers and sisters, in conformity with His image, and in conformity with His own words: "Blessed are the peacemakers, for they will be called sons of God."[57]

8

The Ministry of Reconciliation

In the summer of 1983 I was present as Chuck Colson (the one-time Watergate defendant, now a lay evangelist and prison-reform advocate) addressed an audience of pastors and lay Christians gathered from 134 countries in an event called Amsterdam '83, sponsored by the Billy Graham Evangelistic Association. During his talk Colson told about a recent visit he made with some Christian laymen to the death row of one of America's largest prisons, the Indiana State Penitentiary. Twenty men were there awaiting execution, and with them were 20 Christian volunteers, singing and praying and sharing Jesus Christ.

Two men especially caught Colson's attention as they prayed together. One was an inmate, a convicted murderer, a black man whom we'll call Henry Lewis; he was waiting to die. The other was a Christian volunteer, a white man we'll call Thomas Dodge.

As the group of volunteers was preparing to leave, Colson noticed Henry Lewis and Thomas Dodge going back to Lewis' cell together. Colson followed them into the cell and said to Dodge, "We have to go. The warden is waiting to escort us out of the cell block."

Dodge said, "Chuck, can't you wait a little while longer?"

"We really need to get going," Colson replied. "I have a very tight schedule. Some of us have other appointments."

"Chuck, please," Dodge quietly pleaded, "this is very important. You see, I am Judge Thomas Dodge, and I sentenced this man, Henry Lewis, to die. But since he was placed in this prison he has become a Christian, my brother in the Lord. We just need a few more minutes to forgive each other, and to pray for each other, and to love each other."

In that prison cell stood two men, one black, one white; one was powerless, the other powerful; one was sentenced to die, the other the judge who pronounced sentence. And they stood there, arms wrapped around each other with a love the world doesn't understand. Revival came to the Indiana State Penitentiary in the days that followed, in ways never before seen in the history of that prison.

If God can reconcile Thomas Dodge and Henry Lewis, He can reconcile any of us in the church, no matter what our differences. When the world sees authentic love, reconciling people with incredible differences through Jesus Christ, revival always comes.

Care Enough to Confront

Second Corinthians 5:18,19 tells us that God has not only reconciled us to Himself through Christ, but He has also given us the *ministry* and *message* of reconciliation. The ministry of reconciliation is twofold: 1) it commits to us the task of helping others become reconciled to God, through faith in Jesus Christ; and 2) it places on us the responsibility of living out a life of reconciliation toward our brothers and sisters in the body of Christ.

When we commit ourselves to the ministry of reconciliation, we take a step that involves making ourselves vulnerable to others, as we make ourselves available and obedient to God as His agents of forgiveness, reconciliation, and healing. Sometimes the process of forgiving and reconciling with others is hard— very hard.

There are often times in our lives when we are seriously wronged by another Christian, or when we see a brother or sister falling into a serious error or sin, or when we observe a fellow Christian bringing harm to someone else. At such times, according to Scripture, we have an obligation to courageously go to that person face-to-face and seek to bring about reconciliation and renewed relationship between that person and God, or that person and another Christian, or that person and ourselves.

Our Lord said, "If your brother sins against you, go and show him his fault, just between the two of you. If he listens to you, you have won your brother over."[58] In Galatians 6:1 Paul wrote, "Brothers, if someone is caught in a sin, you who are spiritual should restore him gently. But watch yourself, or you also may be tempted."

When there is an offense between you and another Christian, or when you discover that another Christian is involved in a serious sin which would bring harm to himself or to others, the Bible counsels that you should go to that person directly, in private, just you and him, and *confront* him in love, in gentleness, in humility—not as one who is morally superior, but as one who sincerely cares, recognizing your own fallibility and capacity for sin.

If that person listens to you, then you have helped to heal and reconcile him; you have won him over. The matter is ended. You don't have to tell anyone else or spread any rumors. It never needs to be mentioned again, even between the two of you. It is covered over completely and eternally by Christlike forgiveness.

The Yoke of Christ

Remember especially that all-important word in Galatians 6:1, "gently." In these private conversations with those who are caught in a sin, we need to communicate the fact that we have come to them out of love, not out of self-righteousness; we have confronted them in humility and obedience, not out of arrogance and aggressiveness. We need to let the erring person know that we are on his side, not on his back; that we are praying for him, not judging him. Our biblical mandate is not to accuse and punish, but to gently—*gently!*—call our brother to repentance and healing.

If the virtue of gentleness is explicitly commanded by Paul, then implicit in Galatians 6:1 we see the command to be *humble*: "But watch yourself, or you also may be tempted." Examine yourself, remembering that it could happen to you. Be humble. Be wary of your own capacity for sin.

Did you know that there is only one place in the whole New Testament where Jesus describes His own character? It's in Matthew 11:29—"Take my yoke upon you and learn from me, for I am *gentle* and *humble* in heart." Those same two words again: *gentleness* and *humility*. Romans 8:29 tells us that throughout our lives, our goal in life is to be conformed to the likeness, the character, of Jesus Christ. In Jesus' own words, we are to take His yoke upon ourselves. As we become more like Him, we will become more and more gentle and humble.

If you sense that God is calling you to confront another believer, remember those two words: *gentleness* and *humility*. It is these two Christlike qualities that are particularly crucial in those hard times when God calls us to gently, lovingly confront and restore a brother or sister in Christ.

In my own life I have occasionally had to privately confront someone I knew had become ensnared in a problem with drinking, or child abuse, or a wrong sexual entanglement, or unethical business dealings, or spouse abuse, or spreading rumors, or some other ongoing sin. When I've had the courage to face that person honestly, humbly, prayerfully, obediently with the truth—

which has not been nearly as often as it should have been—it has been difficult for me, it has been painful, it has even been costly in some ways. It goes against the grain of my temperament. But in almost every case, this first step of loving, face-to-face confrontation with the truth has been enough to lead that person to repentance.

What if we have done everything we could to lovingly win our brother or sister over to a restored relationship with ourselves and with God? If that person remains unrepentant, should we then *withhold* forgiveness from him? Absolutely not! We should forgive him continuously and immediately and completely. In fact, we should forgive the person even *before* we go to confront him or her. A sinner's confession and repentance are prerequisites to healing and reconciliation, but not to forgiveness! Forgiveness must be complete and instantaneous and unconditional.

In John 8, Jesus forgave the woman caught in adultery *before* He told her, "Go now and leave your life of sin." He didn't wait for signs of remorse and repentance in her life, nor did He demand an apology and signs of contrition before He forgave those who nailed Him to the cross. So should our forgiveness be. As Christ taught us in the Lord's Prayer, we pardon other people's sins against us because God has already forgiven our sins; we don't forgive others because they say, "I'm sorry."

Qualified to Confront

May God guard us from feeling any sense of superiority to the one who has been caught in an overt act of sin. In our human fallibility and moral blindness, we often tend to single out certain kinds of sin—say, sexual sins or drug abuse—as the worst offenses against God's law.

To this attitude C. S. Lewis replies: "The sins of the flesh are bad, but they are the least bad of all sins. All the worst sins are purely spiritual. The pleasure of putting other people in the wrong, of bossing and patronizing, backbiting and pride. That is why a cold, self-righteous, arrogant person who goes regularly to church may be far nearer to hell than a prostitute.''

The first step before we go to a sinning brother and confront him with his fault is to *examine ourselves*. When we see a fellow Christian involved in a practice or a habit that is likely to be his undoing, or the undoing of the church, we must look inside ourselves and say, "How do I know if I'm *qualified* to confront?"

The apostle Paul gives us these guidelines: "The fruit of the Spirit is love, joy, peace, patience, kindness, goodness, faithfulness, gentleness and self-control. . . . Brothers, if someone is caught in a sin, *you who are spiritual* should restore him gently.''[59]

Who is qualified to confront? *You who are spiritual.* You who have the marks of Christian maturity, the fruit of the Spirit in your character. You are qualified to confront *if* you are experiencing a growing sense of the qualities of a Spirit-controlled character in your life; if you are becoming more and more loving, joyful, at peace, patient, kind, good, faithful, gentle, and self-controlled.

You need to search out *why* you feel called to confront someone else. You should test your life, your obedience, and your motives against the Scriptures, then ask yourself, "Am I a concerned Christian, committed to serving others, lovingly involved in others' lives, or am I an aggressive, meddling, self-appointed busybody, accusing others of assorted wrongs while ignoring the sin and pride of my own life?" He that is spiritual will carefully, prayerfully examine himself, and discern the difference.

Called to Confront

I've made many bad choices in my life, and I'm grateful to God that, throughout my life, there have always been people around me who have had the love and courage to take me aside and help me understand a better way to live. Many times I've been on the receiving end of a gentle, loving confrontation over a mistake or a sin in my life, and it has been totally clear to me that the goal of the person who confronted me was *to help me, not hurt me; to heal me, not cripple me.*

But I have also, through the years, had to endure the kind of harsh, accusing dialogue that damages the human spirit and injures the relationship between Christian brothers and sisters. These hurtful dialogues have taken place in private confrontations, or in front of a group, or in letters (both signed and anonymous), or over the phone.

Reflecting back on these two kinds of confrontation, there's no question in my mind which kind has been more helpful for my growth and maturity. Clearly, anyone will be more open and teachable when he is confronted in gentleness and humility than when he is attacked with strong, aggressive accusations. When we confront a brother or sister in Christ in a spirit of unconditional acceptance and forgiveness, his or her heart is pierced by God's own love, not wounded by the poisoned spear of our own anger and vindictiveness.

Think back for a moment. Is there someone who comes to your mind who has strayed, drifted, sinned, made wrong choices? You may not want the job of confronting that person, but it may well be that God is calling you to love that person back to his rightful place as a child of God. It's not an easy calling, but it's one of the most significant callings in the Christian life. Certainly we must be careful that we are not overly *eager* to confront another Christian. But if God is truly calling us to confront, then we shouldn't run from it either.

May God give us hearts of courage and unconditional love, so that we will care enough to confront and bring about reconciliation. And may we be obedient and loving enough to instantly, continuously, completely *forgive.*

Clearing the Rubble

For many of us, the ministry of reconciliation calls us not so much to confront another Christian as to confront *ourselves,* to look inward, to look back over our past and take stock of ourselves. Of course, we know that if we've committed ourselves to Christ, God has completely forgiven and forgotten our sins. Yet even after we are forgiven and our sins are forgotten, often the rubble of our sins remains strewn about behind us—people we've hurt or angered or offended. Often we have committed acts that have caused relationships to be broken. Those people and those relationships need to be healed, and so do we.

When we sin against others, the way back to wholeness and reconciliation is something called *confession*: "Confess your sins to each other and pray for each other so that you may be healed."[60] If we want to clear the rubble of the past, to be healed, to be whole, we need to have the honesty, integrity, and courage to go to the people we've wronged and confess those wrongs. Confessing our sins to those we've wronged serves several positive functions:

1) Confession brings healing and peace to our own souls, and relieves us of guilt. In *Experiencing God's Forgiveness*, Luis Palau writes, "It is rougher to carry sin with you than to confess it and experience release. Why? Because your burdens collect interest, and they get heavier with each new day. Imagine carrying a horrible weight around your neck for the next fifty years. It is not worth it, my friend. Clear it up and you will be at peace."

2) Confession brings forgiveness from the one we've wronged and brings about reconciliation. In the Sermon on the Mount, Jesus taught us that, in God's eyes, *relationship* is more important than *religion*: "If you are offering your gift at the altar and there remember that your brother has something against you, leave your gift there in front of the altar. First go and be reconciled to your brother; then come and offer your gift."[61]

Is there a brother or sister in Christ who has something against you? Is there someone you've hurt or gossiped about or stolen from or offended? Then God wants you to begin *now* to pray and work toward restoring that relationship. He desires reconciliation between fellow Christians *more* than He desires our various busy acts of religious service.

3) Confession makes us more aware of our sins and how they affect other people. All of us have rough edges in our personalities. Sometimes these rough edges hurt others, and yet we are quick to excuse ourselves. We need to become acutely aware of the fact there are people who are without Christ, who are watching our behavior, looking for Christ's life to be lived out in us—but are going away, shaking their heads, disillusioned. If we confess and reconcile with those we've hurt, we will become more sensitive to their feelings and to the rough edges in our own character. We will become more Christlike.

Confession frees us from guilt, makes us spiritually and emotionally whole, and restores our relationships with each other. Confession brings health to the body of Christ, the church. But remember this: Our acts of confession need not be any more public than the sins we are confessing. If you have hurt a brother, you need to confess your sin to that brother; you're not required to confess it before the entire congregation.

The Bible discloses to us a way to be healed, a way to be reconciled, a way to *be* forgiven and to *feel* forgiven. Love and forgiveness cover a multitude of sins, grievances, wrongs, and differences. God is calling us to be reconciled with each other, to bury our disagreements and grudges, to love unconditionally while it is today, and not to dwell on the grievances of the past.

Many of us have shut our brothers and sisters out of our hearts through acts of unforgiveness, or through proudly refusing to confess our faults. But life is short and hangs by a slender thread; our estranged brother or sister may be snatched away at any moment, and with them our last chance to reconcile and love and forgive each other. How sad it is that we stubbornly choose to add to the tragedy that comes so often and so suddenly in this life by failing to live lives of beautiful reconciliation, of extravagant love.

Our lives can be filled with acts of forgiveness and reconciliation, with wholeness and joy and love—a love that reaches out beyond ourselves and infects our homes, our churches, our communities with the gospel of Jesus Christ, the good news of the forgiveness of sin, of the reconciliation of people to God, and of people to people.

God does not force His will on our will. Rather, He is pleading with us, as He pleaded with the early church through the apostle Paul: "Bear with each other and forgive whatever grievances you may have against one another. Forgive as the Lord forgave you. And over all these virtues put on love, which binds them all together in perfect unity."[62]

The ministry of reconciliation is upon every man and woman who exalts the name of Jesus as Lord and Savior. May we have the love and courage to always seek reconciliation with one another and thereby praise to our God.

9

Forgiven and Unified

Jack was a Christian graduate student at a school in Illinois. Toward the end of the school year he decided he wanted to have a significant ministry for Jesus Christ during the summer break. He considered a number of options: assisting in the youth program of a metropolitan church, or perhaps working with a parachurch ministry such as Young Life or Youth for Christ, or possibly counseling and befriending young people at a Christian summer camp.

So Jack prayed for the Lord to give him such a ministry, but the Lord didn't open any of these options to him. His applications, resumes, and interviews were all met with the same reply: "Sorry, we don't have an opening at this time."

Finally Jack realized that if he were going to have enough

money to even continue his schoolwork in the fall, he was going to have to forget finding a ministry for the summer, and simply find a job—*any* job.

After a couple more weeks of trying, only one job turned up—and not a very attractive job at that. But Jack resigned himself to the fact that, for the next three months, he was going to be a bus driver in that rough, crime-infested ghetto called the South Side of Chicago.

One day while Jack was on his route, he picked up a bunch of teenagers, members of a violent street gang, who readily spotted the fact that he was a young rookie driver, and that he was nervous. So they decided to have a little fun. They refused to pay the fare, and rode for as long as they wanted, while jeering and shouting obscenities at Jack and intimidating the other passengers.

These young gang members had so much fun the first day that they made a point of seeking out Jack's bus the following day, and the day after that, and the day after that. Each day the taunts and threats grew worse. Each day the gang members pushed the situation closer and closer to confrontation. Each day Jack warned them, and each day they answered with curses and jeers.

After about a week of this, Jack decided he had had it. Spotting a police car parked along the street, he pulled over and asked the policeman to come aboard the bus and make the gang members either pay or get off.

The boys paid—and they stayed on.

A few blocks down the street, as Jack pulled the bus to a stop to pick up a fare, the boys surrounded him, pulled him off the bus, and beat him without mercy. They broke several of his ribs, knocked out two of his teeth, and left him unconscious in a puddle of his own blood.

When he came around, he was in an ambulance, on his way to the hospital. In the hospital, and afterward, when he went home to recover, he was bitter, angry, resentful—not only toward those gang members, but toward God.

"God, I asked You for a ministry," he prayed. "I would have

taken *any* ministry. Instead, all You gave me was this lousy job, and a no-choice invitation to a beating. Where were You when I needed Your help, God?''

A few days later Jack decided to press charges against the gang. With the help of some eyewitnesses, the gang was arrested and eventually brought to trial.

During the course of that trial, as Jack sat across the courtroom from his attackers, something strange began to happen. The Holy Spirit began to move in his heart. He began to feel the hatred and resentment that he had felt so deeply for these boys gradually melt into equally strong feelings of compassion and pity and unconditional love.

Finally all of those gang members were found guilty. Just as the judge was about to pronounce sentence, Jack stood up and asked to be heard. ''Your Honor,'' he said, ''I would like you to add up all the days that you are about to sentence these young men to serve in jail, and I would like you to allow me to serve all their time instead.''

There was stunned silence in that courtroom. The judge, the defense attorneys, the prosecuting attorney, and the gallery of witnesses were speechless—but none as much as the convicted assailants. The judge finally found his voice and said, ''Young man, I can't imagine what would motivate you to make such an absurd request! Certainly you know I can never agree to such a thing! It's completely unprecedented!''

''Oh, there's a precedent, all right,'' Jack replied. ''You see, 2,000 years ago, on a hill called Calvary, a man named Jesus Christ took the rap and paid the price for me, and for you, and for everyone in this room. I only ask to be allowed to do the same for these boys.''

The judge, still hardly comprehending the strange request, refused it, and proceeded to sentence the gang members to jail. But Jack went to that jail anyway—as a visitor. He witnessed to those gang members, and eventually saw nearly every one of the boys who had assaulted him won to Christ by his act of unconditional love and forgiveness.

And then Jack saw that God *had* answered his prayers after

all. He had given him a powerful ministry for Jesus Christ—a ministry of forgiveness and reconciliation. And the result was that the Spirit of conviction, the Spirit of revival, swept through the hearts of some of the hardest, toughest young men in the cruelest ghetto of Chicago. Lives were changed for all eternity because one young man was willing to show love in an unlovely situation, and to forgive an act of brutal cruelty.

There is a powerful force that is within our hands right now, a power to change lives, a power to bring revival to the church, a power to demonstrate the reconciling love of Jesus Christ to a world that is dying in sin and despair. That power is *forgiveness*.

Shockwaves of Forgiveness

Forgiveness is a vanishingly rare commodity in the world today.

In January 1984 the world was thunderstruck when it saw that Pope John Paul II had gone to Rebibbia Prison in Rome and offered his pardon to Mehmet Ali Agca, the 26-year-old, Turkish-born terrorist who had tried to kill him a little more than two years earlier. This simple act of forgiveness sent shockwaves through the world's news media, and prompted *Time* magazine to devote a cover and seven full pages of its January 9, 1984, issue to the question "Why Forgive?" In that issue, *Time* senior writer Lance Morrow wrote:

> Christ preached forgiveness, the loving of one's enemies. It is at the center of the New Testament. Stated nakedly, superficially, the proposition sounds perverse and even self-destructive, an invitation to disaster. . . .
>
> Forgiveness is not an impulse that is in much favor. It is a mysterious and sublime idea in many ways. The prevalent style in the world runs more to the high-plains drifter, to the hard, cold eye of the avenger, to a numb remorselessness. Forgiveness does not look much like a tool for survival in a bad world. But that is what it is.

These insightful words accurately state how the world stands on the subject of forgiveness and unconditional love. We live in an unforgiving world—a place where those rare, beautiful acts of pardon and reconciliation stand out like blossoms among the crabgrass.

God intended that the church would stand apart as a haven of love and forgiveness in a sea of hostility and despair. Yet all too often we in the church have absorbed and displayed the values of the unforgiving world around us rather than the unconditional love of God. We need to take a fresh look at ourselves and our relationships with one another in the church, the body of Christ. We need to gain God's perspective.

The Last Will and Testament of Jesus Christ

The Holy Spirit is waiting to be unleashed on the world, to bring about a revolution of love and changed lives and saving grace, but throughout the world He is being hindered by Christians battling each other, dwelling on grudges, spreading gossip, and bearing malice. I once saw Luis Palau, that great Latin American evangelist, stand before a crowd of churchmen and churchwomen, with tears in his eyes, saying, "Everywhere I go the harvest is *ripe*, but everywhere I go, Christians are *fighting*!"

How it must break the heart of the Lord! Just before He was betrayed and crucified, Jesus prayed to the Father *especially* for the church that was to follow Him, *especially* for you and me as believers. And His one request—in effect, His last will and testament—was for *unity* between fellow Christians.

Three times in that prayer Jesus prays for our unity: "...that all of them may be *one*, Father, just as you are in me and I am in you...that they may be *one* as we are one...may they be brought to complete *unity* to let the world know that you sent me."[63] Even before He went to the cross, Jesus planned for the world to come to know Him *through our unity*. The harvest is ripe, but Christians are fighting, and the heart of God is broken.

"You will receive power when the Holy Spirit comes on you,"

said the risen Christ to His disciples just before He ascended, "and you will be my witnesses in Jerusalem, and in all Judea and Samaria, and to the ends of the earth."[64] Jesus has called *each* of us, without exception, to be His witnesses wherever we are—at school, at work, in our neighborhoods. And what are we witnesses to? We are to bear witness that Jesus was sent from God the Father, that He was sacrificed for our sins, that He rose again for our eternal life, that through Him we have forgiveness of sin!

We bring the world a *gospel of forgiveness!*

But how can we *preach* forgiveness if we are not willing to *practice* forgiveness? If we preach forgiveness while we practice malice and gossip and grudge-bearing, we shame the gospel and dishonor the last wishes of our Lord before He went to His death for us. There must be congruence between our talk and our walk, or else our talk means nothing.

Acts of Unforgiveness

The church is the one place of all places that should be a *fellowship of forgiveness*—where we find an overflowing expression of the grace, love, acceptance, encouragement, and forgiveness of God. Tragically, our churches are all too often places where the precise *opposite* qualities are expressed in superabundance.

In church after church, acts of unforgiving *anger* arise over issues of doctrine and Scripture interpretation. Over and over, fits of unforgiving *rage* flare up over some minor insult, whether real or imagined, by one brother toward another. Unforgiving *gossip* spreads through a church like fire through dry grass, destroying reputations and breaking relationships. Often, *grudges* and *malice* seethe for years, so that two brothers or sisters in Christ come to church Sunday after Sunday, hear the same sermons, sing the same hymns, partake of the same table of communion, pray "forgive us our debts as we forgive our debtors"—and yet they sit on opposite sides of the aisle, never looking at each other, never speaking, all because of some old wound in their relationship that has never been healed and forgiven.

These acts of unforgiveness are nothing new in the church. Throughout his ministry, in letter after letter to church after church, the apostle Paul battled crises of division and hard-hearted unforgiveness. He warned, coaxed, encouraged, confronted, urged, and pleaded with people to just love and accept and forgive one another, to unite with one another, to be *one* as our Lord intended.

Throughout the New Testament are veritable "shopping lists" of unforgiving acts and attitudes: Romans 16; 1 Corinthians 1, 11, and 12; Galatians 5; Ephesians 4; Philippians 2; and Colossians 3. Here are found stern and uncompromising warnings against sins that most of us tend to take pretty much for granted, sins that many of us consider "minor."

Galatians 5:19-26 gives us God's perspective on these so-called "minor" sins: They are called "acts of the sinful nature," and thus they are totally inconsistent with the Spirit-led life. We are commanded to live by the Spirit, to begin living out the fruit of the Spirit—"love, joy, peace, patience, kindness, goodness, faithfulness, gentleness and self-control"—so that we will cease to gratify the desires of the sinful nature. The acts of the sinful nature and the fruit of the Spirit cannot cohabit the same life; one must ultimately destroy the other.

Among the unforgiving acts of the sin nature are:

Rage: Sudden, untempered outbursts of anger. If you are given to losing your temper, to fits of rage, then it's time to stop excusing yourself. It's time to stop saying, "That's just the way I am. I get mad fast, and I get over it fast. People just have to understand that about me." No, God *commands* us to get rid of rage, to put it to death, to cast it out of our character, and to replace it with gentleness and compassion and forgiveness.[65]

Malice: Evil thoughts, wishing harm toward others, dwelling on our anger toward others—even rejoicing when evil befalls someone else. Malice and forgiveness are mutually exclusive. Malice delights in evil, but forgiving love, says 1 Corinthians 13:6, does not delight in evil but rejoices with the truth.[66]

Bitterness: In the Greek New Testament the word for bitterness connotes a heart turned willfully hard, obdurate, cold. A bitter person rejects the path of forgiveness by a stubborn bent of his will. God's command to us is that bitterness must be cast out of our hearts.[67]

Slander: Also known as gossip or bearing false witness or spreading an evil report. Gossip is an insidious, pervasive sin in the church. It seldom matters whether the gossip being spread is an outright lie or the factual truth; indeed, the so-called "truth," when cruelly and maliciously targeted, can be as sinful and destructive as the most outrageous lie. We often rationalize, excuse, or laugh off this sin, but the Bible soberly condemns gossip as a serious act of unforgiveness.[68]

Filthy language: This is a more common and deeply rooted problem in the church than most of us will admit. In fact, many Christians today treat this clearly condemned sin as a matter of "Christian freedom," blithely viewing others who are shocked or offended by their language as "legalistic" or "puritanical." But the Scriptures are clear: Whenever we use profanity in a moment of anger or frustration, or casually in our speech, or when we treat others with vile names of contempt, we display the unforgiving acts of the sinful nature.[69] "Out of the same mouth come praise and cursing," laments James 3:10. "My brothers, this should not be!"

Hatred: The person who hates is the person who has set himself in opposition to the central qualities that the gospel of Jesus Christ engenders in the human heart: forgiveness, peace, reconciliation, and unconditional love. Hatred is *war* on a person-to-person basis. The one who hates brings hostility and strife into the body of Jesus Christ (Galatians 5:20).

Jealousy, envy, selfish ambition: Sometimes the sin of jealousy arises when we covet something good, something true. Some of us envy the spiritual gifts of another. Some of us envy another person's ministry, his popularity as a pastor or teacher, or his administrative or organizing skills. Watch your attitude toward those you have a tendency to envy. Watch for the appearance of ambitious envy, egotistical pride, or covetous jealousy that so often leads to backbiting, malice, and bitterness.[70]

Discord and dissension: Do you take pleasure in arguing for argument's sake? Do you delight in provoking dissension? Then you are committing acts of unforgiveness that bring division to the body of Christ, and grief to the Holy Spirit.[71]

Factions: Do you side with one party or another in your church, or do you instead seek to be a catalyst for reconciliation between people who are struggling with each other? We are many parts, but we are *one* body. If you have set yourself as a member of "one side" in the church, in opposition to the "other side," then you have become part of a faction; you have committed an act of unforgiveness.[72]

Brawling: Open conflict, arguing, heated verbal exchanges between believers. The act of unforgiveness that the Bible calls "brawling" is an open scandal, bringing shame to the gospel of Jesus Christ, the gospel of peace, the gospel of reconciliation.[73]

These unforgiving acts of the sin nature have no place in the church of Jesus Christ, where they bring division, damage lives, hinder ministry, and call down disgrace on the gospel. "Those who belong to Christ Jesus have crucified the sinful nature with its passions and desires," says Galatians 5:24,25. "Since we live by the Spirit, let us keep in step with the Spirit."

Forgiven and Unified

We are the fellowship of the forgiven. We serve a God of forgiveness. We have a gospel of forgiveness to give to the world.

So why are we in the church not unified?

God can create the universe from nothing. He can heal diseases and resurrect the dead. But there is one thing He chooses in His sovereignty *not* to do: He will not run roughshod over our will. If we are open and surrendered to His will, seeking to crucify the sinful nature and purge its unforgiving acts from our lives, He will use us, He will work through us. But if we resist Him, if we choose *not* to reconcile with our other brothers and sisters in Christ, if we choose to live out the acts of the sinful nature toward our fellow Christians, then He is *hindered* from working. It's as simple as that.

God calls us to live out the fruit of the Spirit, to forgive and reconcile with our brothers and sisters, to be *one* in the body of Christ. This usually sounds simple enough until we're confronted with a *specific* situation which calls for us to show unconditional love and forgiveness.

To practice unconditional, instantaneous, complete forgiveness toward one another takes obedient, moment-by-moment surrender of the will. To cast the acts of unforgiveness out of our lives takes continuous reliance upon God. To be reconciled with another brother or sister takes humility, wisdom, and considerable courage.

But if we are not willing to take these steps of obedience, forgiveness, and reconciliation—in short, if we are not willing to be *unified* with every other person who names the name of Christ—then we have *no right* to preach a gospel of forgiveness to an unforgiving world. If we choose not to practice the gospel we preach, then our preaching is worth precisely nothing.

God has been showing me from His Word that *unity* is the prelude to Pentecost, the prerequisite to the power of the Holy Spirit. He has been convicting me of the fact that, guided by His Spirit and in His timing, I need to seek to completely mend any broken relationships in my life.

There is an enormous risk in these words; I don't write them lightly. The risk is this: I am going on record, committing myself to live out what I am saying here. As I write this I am examining my own heart, and I have a confession to make: There are individuals within my own church, my own family of faith, with whom I need to do some work in order to bring about reconciliation. To the degree that I hold back in seeking total reconciliation, I am being a hindrance to allowing the Holy Spirit to be poured out in my own church. I know this, and I am committed to changing it.

Will you join me in that commitment?

If there is one person from whom you are withholding forgiveness and acts of reconciliation, then you should know that *you* are hindering the Holy Spirit from working in your life, and from infusing His power in your church and in your community. It's your responsibility; you can't hide from it.

"I urge you to live a life worthy of the calling you have received," implores the apostle Paul in Ephesians 4:1-3. "Be completely humble and gentle; be patient, bearing with one another in love. Make every effort to keep the unity of the Spirit through the bond of peace."

10

The Forgiving Family

"Son! Son, don't walk away while I'm talking to you!"

"*Walk* away, Dad? I'm *running* away! I'm going as fast and as far away from here as I can go! Just try and stop me! I dare you! Just try!"

And while this rebellious teenage boy stormed out the front door, his mother stood helplessly by, crying and wringing her hands. "Stop him," she sobbed to her husband. "Don't let him go!"

"Stop him? How? Nothing I say gets through to him!"

Suddenly they heard from the garage the slam of a car door, followed by the angry roar of the engine and the squeal of rubber. Dashing out onto the front porch, this father and mother watched helplessly as their son crashed the family car backward through the closed garage door. He continued roaring backward down the drive and onto the street. At high speed he backed completely around the block, tires screeching at every corner, and returned to the house. The car careened over the mailbox and across the lawn, finally coming to rest atop a brick-lined flower bed.

The boy turned off the engine, leaped out of the car, and flung the keys at his father. "That's what I think of your religion, Dad! All my life you've been trying to stuff religion down my throat! I've had it! I'm leaving! I'm going someplace where I don't have to listen to any more sermons from you!"

And with that he turned and walked away from his heart-broken parents.

If we're honest, we have to admit that, with variations in detail, this kind of scene is played out in thousands of Christian homes these days. Tragically, broken parent-child relationships are all too common in the church of the 1980s, in good homes, in the families of church members, elders, deacons, pastors, and missionaries. Across this country, moms and dads offer broken-hearted prayers of, "*Why*, Lord? *How* did we fail as parents? *Why* did this happen?"

Certainly there are many factors, great and small, that lead to brokenness in family relationships, including many factors which are outside a parent's control. Yet in all too many cases, relationships between marriage partners, and between parents and children, are needlessly damaged by a parent's unwillingness to exhibit love without conditions, to model forgiveness, and to seek reconciliation.

I believe the Christian family can be made stronger, more durable for the hard trials of life, more accepting and affirming of its children, and more completely what God intended it to be, if only we will look to the blueprint for the family that God has given us in His Word.

A Thousand Single Steps

Though most of us can point to a few truly decisive moments in our lives—a dramatic conversion to Christ or a cataclysmic event that opened our understanding to some working of God's will—the job of Christian parenting is primarily and overwhelmingly accomplished through a gradual, day-by-day, moment-by-moment process, a process of a thousand single steps.

Probably the most sudden, dramatic encounter anyone ever had with Jesus Christ was the apostle Paul's conversion on the road to Damascus. As Paul himself described it, Christ appeared to him in a blazing, blinding light and said, "Why do you persecute me? It is hard for you to kick against the goads!"[74] It was as if Jesus were saying to Paul, "Why are you resisting Me? Why are you resisting the goads, the hundreds of circumstances I have been bringing into your life to drive you to Me?" Even in the sudden, momentous conversion of Paul, there had been many single steps of preparation of the heart.

And so it is with us as parents, and with our kids.

We need to understand that the qualities we want to build in our children do not come about in some once-in-a-lifetime moment of profound dialogue with them. They do not come only in some future dramatic moment of self-discovery or summer-camp dedication. They come through a process of a thousand single steps of loving, caring, touching, discipling, and modeling of acceptance, unconditional love, and forgiveness. Wholeness in family relationships comes about through a dedicated, lifelong *strategy* of teaching and honestly living out the Christian faith and the Christian walk *daily*, right before our children's keen and watchful eyes.

It has been said that in the family, forgiveness and the love of Jesus Christ are not so much *taught* as they are *caught*. In some ways this is a hard fact to face. It means that we have to live what we say we believe. Our kids see us every day, through all kinds of sorrows, pressures, frustrations, anger, doubt, and conflict. They know the hypocrisy that underlies the words, "Don't do what I *do*, do what I *say*!"

But if we commit ourselves to the strategy of nurturing our children through a process of a thousand single steps, we will begin to see that the great amount of time we are together with our children is really the one best thing our families have going for them. If we are conscious of the fact that our faith is being *caught* by our children—not just being taught to them—then we can rejoice in the fact that our life in front of our kids is an open book!

When we adopt the strategy of a thousand single steps, things that were once insignificant now take on transcendent importance. We begin to see each new day as a wonderful gift from God, a gift He has given us to use in the process of building love and self-esteem and forgiveness into the character of those beloved children, and of leading them to authentic faith in Jesus Christ.

A friend of mine is married and has three children. He has begun a practice in his family that would be good for all of us dads to adopt. In addition to teaching his children to pray daily, to memorize Scripture, and to attend church and Sunday school, he makes a point once a month of taking one of his children on an outing, just he and that individual child. Each child in turn has his or her own special time of sharing moments and interests and private thoughts, and of being affirmed by Dad.

One summer my friend took his oldest boy, his nine-year-old son, on a canoe trip. They had been out on the lake for a while, had set up camp, and had gotten a campfire going. They were roasting hot dogs and talking and laughing, when suddenly that nine-year-old boy put his arm around his dad's shoulder and said simply, "Boy, Dad, I sure love you!" And my friend hugged his little boy and said, "Son, I sure love you too."

"And you know, Ron," my friend said after telling me about this father-son camping trip, "a moment like that is worth more to me than all the Pee-Wee League home runs and A + report cards I could ever hope for." It is a simple memory, an incalculably *golden* memory, and just one of a thousand single steps my friend is taking to build a relationship, to build trust, to build love in his Christ-centered family.

Modeling Forgiveness

This is not to say that the family is some idyllic utopia of woodland outings and warm hugs and tender emotions. Because we live so close to each other in our families, because we share our lives together in the same house, the home is often a place of conflict, of struggle, and of anger. Some of us may be tempted to simply accept these hard times as natural, as part of any family's ups and downs; others of us may find such times of conflict and anger as times of discouragement, pain, and disillusionment. But probably the best perspective to have on the hard times in family life is to see them as opportunities for *growth*, for *learning*, for *modeling forgiveness*.

We try to teach our children to love others, to generously share with others, to moderate their attitude and actions in trying situations, to forgive and ask forgiveness. But do they see us modeling these virtues, or do they just hear us talk? Our actions speak loudly. The life we live must have congruence with the words we speak, or our words will be proved false and worthy to be ignored or rejected.

We can't model the Christian life, the life of forgiving and being forgiven, by putting on an act, by making an outward show of our values. Our children know what's real and what's phony in our lives. They live too close to us to be fooled. We need to concentrate on *really* building Christlike character in our lives, in living for Jesus Christ even when we think no one is watching. Our kids won't have any reason to believe in our God until they can see that He is really living in us, changing the way we respond to frustration, to trials, to anger, and even to their own acts of disobedience and misbehavior.

If we want to raise children of forgiveness, then we need to be parents of forgiveness, who daily pray to and listen to and serve a God of forgiveness. We need to model our forgiveness after His. Only then will our children model their forgiveness after ours.

Do you make your children or your mate *pay* for forgiveness? Do you make sure they suffer for what they did before you "graciously" grant forgiveness? Do you "stew" for a while, making sure your anger settles like a cloud of tension over the whole house, before you grudgingly say, "All right, then, I'll forgive you *this* time—but it better not happen again"? Do you "forgive" your children's disobedient acts at one time, then naggingly remind them of those same supposedly "forgiven" misdeeds later?

The forgiveness we must build into our lives, and which we seek to model to our children, must be *free*. It must be *immediate*. It must be *final* and *continuous*. We must forgive and forget. That is what the forgiveness of Christ is like. So must our forgiveness be.

Our children learn more from our lives than from our words. What are we teaching them?

Let Your Kids Forgive You

Perhaps you are already striving to be a model to your children. That's good—but are you trying *too* hard? Are you trying to model *perfection* to your children? A lot of us are afraid to admit our mistakes to our kids, to crack that false facade of imitation perfection, lest they lose respect for us. Deep down we know that the image we're trying to project is a *false front*. But understand this: You will *never* convince your family that you don't make mistakes. All you will prove to your family is that you never *admit* mistakes.

I urge you to stop trying to live a lie before your kids. You don't need to model "perfection" before them. In fact, you *can't*; it just isn't humanly possible. You need to communicate to your children that your *goal* as a Christian parent is to glorify God, to become like Christ, and to live a Spirit-controlled life of love and forgiveness. And you need to communicate that this is your goal *even when you fail to achieve it*. In those times when you fail, you need to seek God's forgiveness and your children's forgiveness, confessing your human fallibility, receiving forgiveness, and seeking reconciliation.

You may be thinking, "What will my kids think of me if I say I'm sorry? Will they think I'm weak? Will they find out I make mistakes? Will I lose their respect?" These are all the wrong questions. The *real* question when we make mistakes with our kids—either through anger or an unfair decision or even through good intentions—is this: "Am I mature enough and secure enough in Christ to confess my mistakes to my family, knowing that this will really *cement* the bonds of trust and love and respect with them?"

You see, anyone can preach to his or her kids and tell them how they ought to forgive others and how they ought to ask forgiveness when they do wrong. But while we're preaching to our kids, we may well be failing to live out that kind of forgiveness in our day-to-day relationship with them. Our kids can see that hypocrisy in us, and they won't be fooled for long.

My father was a very gentle-natured, even-tempered man, the pastor of a small church in Iowa. I remember one time when I was a little boy, Dad became very angry with my brother Paul and me over something we had done. In fact, he probably over-reacted in this situation. He yelled at us, then stormed out of the house, slamming the front door behind him. I'd never seen him so angry before or since.

We lived in a parsonage, right across the street from the church, and I remember looking out the window and watching him walk across the street and into the darkened, empty sanctuary of that church. He stayed there for about two hours. I don't know what he was doing in there for two hours, but my hunch is that he was sitting in one of those pews, praying to God and struggling with his feelings of anger and with self-reproach over his own reaction toward us.

I can remember my own feelings that night with crystal clarity. I was especially miserable in that I had been the cause of my father—my gentle, even-tempered father—losing his temper in a way I had *never* seen before. I went to bed that night before Dad came home, and I lay there in the dark, wide awake, for what seemed like an awfully long time.

Then I remember my bedroom door swinging silently open, and the light from the hallway spilling into the darkness of my room, and my Dad stood silhouetted in the doorway for a moment. In that moment there must still have been a struggle going on in his heart; I know that what he was doing couldn't have been easy for him. But he did it: He came to my bedside and knelt there and said, "Son, forgive me. I was wrong."

I was a little boy then. Today I'm a father, with a boy and a girl of my own. My memory of my Dad's beautiful act of reconciliation and love is as vivid today as when it happened, and I'm trying to live out that kind of love in my own family. It took enormous strength and maturity for my Dad to come to me and ask my forgiveness, and that is just one of a thousand things I respect about my Dad's memory.

Our kids will remember and respect their memories of us if we are big enough, strong enough, mature enough to go to our knees in prayer, and to go to them to ask forgiveness. I feel very sorry for any parent—and especially for a father—who is too proud to be wrong, and to admit it, and to ask his family's forgiveness at those times.

My brother Paul has a close and living relationship with Jesus Christ. He and I have talked together about our years together as kids growing up in Iowa, sons of a pastor, raised in the Christian faith. We agreed that there was a time, when we were very young, when we simply accepted what we were taught, and didn't know there was anything else to believe. But we also found that for both of us there came a time in our young adulthood when we questioned the faith of our parents, when we said to ourselves, "I'm going to have to choose either to believe what my parents believe, or I'm going to have to believe something else." And both of us recall that all the difference in our decisions was made by this fact: We saw our parents live out what they said they believed.

Your kids will come to the same moment of decision. Life today offers many choices besides faith in Jesus Christ. There's hedonism, the cult of self and materialism; there's humanism; there are drugs and other destructive enticements; there are false cults and spurious religions waiting to suck up and destroy the minds of confused young people. What will your kids choose?

I believe that you can teach your kids all about Jesus and the

Golden Rule, quote the entire New Testament from memory, and explain the evidence for the resurrection and all the difficult concepts from predestination to the Trinity, but if you're not able to live out *forgiveness*, if you're not able to ask forgiveness from your children when you're wrong, then your children are going to throw your faith right out the window. I think you can pretty well count on that.

My brother and I can well remember one special night in our lives when our Dad came to us and said, "I was wrong. I'm sorry. Please forgive me." And when the time came for Paul and me to make a choice—to decide to make our faith authentically ours, not just something we had been taught—we chose the faith that had given our Dad the strength and maturity to seek forgiveness.

11
Discipline and Forgiveness

Sam Keene tells of the last visit he had with his father at the side of his deathbed. Sam knelt beside his father and said these words: "Dad, you've always been there whenever any of us children needed you. And across the years, you've given us one of the greatest gifts any parent could give. You took delight in us, Dad. In all sorts of ways, you let us know that you were glad we were here, that we had value in your eyes, that our presence was a joy, not a burden to you. You took delight in us."

I believe that, next to knowing Christ, nothing will bring more security to a child than knowing he brings sheer delight to his parents.

Author and speaker Lyman Coleman was planning a vacation with his family. The day before they were to leave on vacation, some business came up and Coleman was unable to go.

But he convinced his wife that she and the kids should take the station wagon and go ahead without him, and he would take a plane to join them the following week.

Three days after they left, he realized he was going to be able to wrap up his business early. Most people would have simply called their family at the motel and said they were on their way. Not this father!

He figured out on the map where his family would be at that time. He took a plane to that city, then took a bus out to the freeway. Standing on a hill overlooking the freeway, clad in a sweatshirt and blue jeans, he waited till he saw the family station wagon, then jumped down to the roadside and stuck out his thumb, hitchhiker-style.

As his family approached in the car, one of the kids said, "That looks like Daddy!" Another yelled out, "That *is* Daddy!" They pulled off the road and stopped. Dad ran up and hugged his wife and kids, and they took off on their vacation together.

Someone later asked Coleman, "Why did you do such a crazy stunt?"

And he said, "For my kids! When I'm gone, I want my kids to remember that their Dad was a lot of fun!" That's a father who delights in his children, who *enjoys* his children.

Blueprint for the Family

The Bible offers a strategy, a blueprint for the family that is idealistic and exalted, and yet at the same time totally practical and applicable. In its pages we can discern God's blueprint for the family as a place where moms and dads nurture and enjoy their kids, and children learn how to love, accept, and forgive others through the love, acceptance, and forgiveness of their parents.

Over the years I've heard a lot of teaching and preaching on the subject of Colossians 3:20—"Children, obey your parents in everything, for this pleases the Lord." Yet I've heard almost *no* teaching at all on the very next verse. Indeed, I believe Colossians 3:21 to be one of the most ignored verses in all of the New Testament's teaching on the Christian home.

In the New International Version that verse reads, "Fathers, do not embitter your children, or they will become discouraged." The New American Standard Bible says, "Fathers, do not exasperate your children, that they may not lose heart."

In the original Greek, that word "fathers" literally means "parents," moms and dads. What does the apostle Paul mean when he warns, "Moms and dads, don't embitter your children, don't exasperate your children, or they'll become discouraged and lose heart"?

I believe we exasperate or embitter our children when we fail in four areas: 1) When we fail to *enjoy* our children; 2) when we *punish* our children, while failing to lovingly *discipline* them; 3) when we fail to make our children feel *affirmed* and unconditionally *accepted*; and 4) when we fail to give them our *time*.

Discipline or Punish?

I've seen many Christian parents who, quite justifiably, have reacted against the permissiveness that produced such a generation of rebellious youth in the '60s and '70s. These parents emphasize discipline, and rightly so, for Hebrews 12:5-11 teaches that an undisciplined child will feel like an unwanted child. But the Bible also points us to a critical *balance* between correction of our children and caring for our children. As Dr. James Dobson says, the Bible encourages us to "shape the will without breaking the spirit" of our children.

As one who has counseled many parents of troubled children, I have to say that I see two principal dangers, two traps that Christian parents are prone to fall into as they try to be biblical in raising and disciplining their children: 1) They fail to understand the spirit in which discipline should be administered according to Scripture; and 2) they fail to perceive that there are other ingredients in child-rearing beyond discipline. I believe that if we are not sensitive to this twofold danger, we will provoke our children, and they will become discouraged.

The first trap: We discipline in the wrong *spirit*. I see three possible tempers or spirits in which most Christian parents administer discipline in their homes:

1) The *permissive* spirit. "Discipline" which takes the form of timid or halfhearted requests for good behavior from children is not discipline at all. This spirit of discipline usually derives from the hazy humanistic notion that people are essentially good, and that our good little kids will grow up into good adults if we're careful not to stifle them or chasten them or suppress their creative urges. But this attitude isn't biblical, it doesn't work, and it doesn't guide children toward responsibility and emotional maturity.

2) The *authoritarian* spirit. Discipline administered in this spirit does not work either. Its motto is, "You do what I say because I say so!" Children disciplined in an authoritarian spirit are not being encouraged toward emotional maturity.

One of the problems with the authoritarian spirit of discipline is that it often results in discipline through *anger*. The parent who responds to his child's behavior with an outpouring of rage will embitter his child, and his child will become discouraged.

3) The *sensitive* spirit. Discipline administered in a spirit of sensitivity is firm, but loving, gracious, consistent, and understanding of the child's emotional needs. This kind of discipline takes place within a larger context of daily affirmation and affection, and helps to shape and guide the child toward emotional maturity.

Discipline that is sensitive is discipline that is gracious. In Colossians 4:6 the apostle Paul tells us that in all our relationships our conversation should be *gracious*. And most of us do maintain graciousness in our relationships with acquaintances and strangers—but what about with our family? How much easier it is for so many of us to show kindness and consideration, gracious concern, and even love for people we hardly know than for our wife, our husband, our children!

The second trap: We fail to understand that there are other ingredients in child-rearing beyond discipline. One of the great tragedies of the last two decades is that thousands of Christian parents, in their eagerness and zeal to be biblically faithful in disciplining their children and in their intense reaction against the permissiveness all around them, have concluded that if they would just be sure to discipline *often* enough and *sternly* enough, their kids would turn out all right. Nothing could be further from the truth.

Properly understood, biblically understood, *discipline* is not simply inflicting unpleasant consequences on our kids in return for their bad behavior. Rather, discipline, as it is described in the Bible, is a process of guiding, shaping, correcting, affirming, loving, and nurturing our children.

A tender young child who grows up under the guidance of firm, loving, Christian discipline will be a child whose will has been shaped and molded into something beautiful. A tender young child who is subjected to a life of punishment will grow to be broken in spirit, broken in self-image, and broken in his relationship to family, friends, and God.

One of the most insightful books ever written about raising, loving, and discipling children is Dr. Ross Campbell's *How to Really Love Your Child*. In that book Dr. Campbell writes:

> Anyone can beat a child with a rod as the primary way of controlling his behavior. That takes no sensitivity, no judgment, no understanding, and no talent. To depend on corporal punishment as the principal method of discipline is to make that critical error in assuming that discipline equals punishment. Discipline is *training* the child in the way he should go. Punishment is only one part of this, and the less the better. Please remember this statement: *the better disciplined a child is, the less punishment will be required*. How well a child responds to discipline depends primarily on how much the child feels loved and accepted. So our biggest task is to make him feel loved and accepted.[75]

How have we Christians so mistakenly and tragically come to view discipline only in the narrow terms of *punishment*? As with most errors that creep into our beliefs and actions as Christians, I believe the central problem is a lack of thoroughness, integrity, and honesty in our approach to Scripture.

Those Christians who loudly advocate physical punishment while failing to adequately emphasize love, acceptance, affirmation and forgiveness usually cite a very few passages in Proverbs to support their claims, such as Proverbs 13:24; 23:13,14; 29:15. "Spare the rod and spoil the child," that trite and shallow slogan of the punishment proponents, is a narrowly focused paraphrase of these verses. Dr. Campbell properly notes the failure of the advocates of "the rod" to take into account the broader, deeper, greater truth that is found throughout the Scriptures. He writes:

> Few plead for a child and his real needs. Too many today are dogmatically calling for children to be punished, calling it discipline, and recommending the harshest, most extreme form of human treatment. Most perplexing of all, many of these advocates call this a biblical approach. . . . They neglect to mention the hundreds of Scripture verses dealing with love, compassion, sensitivity, understanding, forgiveness, nurturing, guidance, kindness, affection, and giving, as though the child has little or no right to these expressions of love.
>
> Proponents of corporal punishment seem to have forgotten that the shepherd's rod referred to in Scripture was used almost exclusively for *guiding* the sheep, especially the lambs, by simply holding the rod to block them from going in the wrong direction and then gently nudge them toward the right direction. If the rod was (or is) an instrument used principally for beating, I would have a difficult time with Psalm 23—"Thy rod and Thy staff, they comfort me" (p. 85).

Biblically, our job as parents is not simply to *control* our children's behavior, but to guide and train our children in the instruction of the Lord, building strong, loving, forgiving, Christlike character in them.

Our goal as Christian parents should be to prepare our children to grow to become men and women who will make a loving difference for Christ in an unloving world. If that goal is always before us, then our children will come to know who God is as they come to know the kind of Christians we are. "As a father has compassion on his children," says Psalm 103:13, "so the Lord has compassion on those who fear Him." Whether we are good examples or bad, our kids look to find God being lived out in us.

Building Cathedrals

One of the things I tell our children regularly, especially if I've been away on a trip for a day or two, is, "One of the things I've missed for the last couple days is just watching the character that God is building into your life. It's so good to be back home with you, and to see that happening in your life."

At other times I take my children aside and hug them close so no one else can hear, and I say something like, "The biggest surprise of my life has been how much *fun* it is to have you as my daughter, my son." Or, "My life would never be the same again if I ever lost you, and I know that I'm a better person because of your life, and the things God teaches me through you." Or, "No matter what you do, I will *always* love you."

Sometimes our children have qualities and character strengths that we haven't mastered as well in our own lives. We need to tell our kids that we are learning and growing by watching their lives. We need to build their self-esteem, their self-worth—not through empty praise or flattery, but by finding their real gifts and strengths, and then *affirming* those qualities in them. We need to be extravagant in our affection toward our kids and take sheer delight in them out of a spirit of gratitude, knowing that they are gifts from God and that we are stewards of those special gifts.

One of my favorite stories is that of the medieval "sidewalk superintendent" who was watching work on a great stone and glass construction project going up in his village. He asked three stonemasons who were working on the project what they were doing. The first replied, "I'm laying bricks." The second said, "I'm building a wall." But the third laborer demonstrated the genuine esteem he had for his work as he smiled and replied, "Me? Why, I'm building a *cathedral*!"

How do you view the job of rearing children? Are you just "laying bricks"? Are you just paying the bills, buying food and clothing, sending them off to school? Or are you building *cathedrals* out of the lives of your children? Are you simply demanding obedience from your children, or are you affirming, loving, forgiving, training, and nurturing your children, raising them up as special handiworks of God, molding them and guiding them into an image that is exalted and Christlike? May the Spirit of God give us the vision to see that we are not just "laying bricks," but that as parents we are called to be *building cathedrals.*

Crisis in the Family

Chet is a man I've known for several years. During that time I've observed him in various dealings with his junior-high-age son, again and again. And in all the times I've seen him with his boy, I've never once seen him respond or conduct himself in any way but with *rage*. He barks orders to his boy, has no patience with his questions, and responds to his most minor failings and mistakes with anger, abusive language, and even physical abuse. My heart has gone out to this young boy whom I've seen alternately humiliated, intimidated, reproached, embittered, fearful, or uncontrollably crying.

I know Chet believes he is being faithful to his responsibility as a parent. But I'm certain that he is his child, and that this boy—a boy with potential, with eagerness to learn, eagerness to please, and an intense need to be loved and affirmed—is in the process of becoming more and more discouraged.

I agree with Dr. James Dobson, who warns that "the most common and costly error in disciplining children is the use of anger in attempting to control our sons and daughters." Today there is a crisis in our American families, and even in our

Christian families. It's a crisis of anger, of rage, of abuse, of secret violence behind our neighbors' doors, behind *our* doors. Many of us as parents are punishing our children in anger, responding in rage, and battering our children emotionally— and often battering them physically. Our children are growing up broken in spirit, broken in self-image, bitter, discouraged, wounded, filled with despair.

The home, which God instituted as the one place of all places where people, and especially children, can find love and acceptance and forgiveness and spiritual nurturing, is today a *battleground*. Domestic violence is commonplace in America today.

And I can tell you that, having seen and talked to and prayed with many of the suffering casualties of these family wars, I know that child abuse and spouse abuse know no boundaries of class or educational background or income bracket or race or faith. One of the best-kept secrets in the American church is the amount of violence occurring within churchgoing families.

I know without any doubt that some of the people reading this book are struggling with tendencies toward rage, toward physical abuse of their families. Perhaps you are struggling with the awful guilt of your own violence toward your spouse or your children. You feel you can't talk about it with anyone, yet you know you have a problem that won't go away without help. You love your mate. You love your children. Yet there are times when you just can't seem to control what you are doing to them.

You need to *show* them that you really do love them. You need to take a big step toward ending the war in your family. You need to find someone you can trust—a pastor, a counselor—to talk to about it; someone who can guide you and help you find insight into controlling your anger, your impulses, your behavior; someone who can pray with you and open God's Word to you and help you to find His power for your weakness, and His forgiveness for your sin. For your sake, for your family's sake, for the sake of your precious children, don't try to do it alone.

Don't Find Time—Make Time!

A little boy went to his father one weekend and asked, "Dad, will you come out to the backyard and help me build a treehouse?"

And this father replied, "Sure, son—but later, okay? Maybe next weekend. You see, I'm really busy right now, but we'll build that treehouse real soon."

"Okay, Dad."

And this boy went to his Dad the next weekend, and on many other weekends, always asking the same hopeful question, always receiving the same well-intentioned answer.

One day this little boy was playing ball in his front yard with some neighbor kids. The ball rolled into the street, and this boy went rushing after it, and was struck by a car. As this little boy lay dying in the hospital, one of the last things he said to his father was, "Well, Dad, I guess we'll never get to build that treehouse."

I officiated at that little boy's funeral. I talked with his grieving father, and I saw him reproach himself, over and over, for his failure to *make time* from his busy schedule to build a relationship with his boy, to enjoy his son, to take pleasure in doing things with him.

Regardless of our stage in life, we can begin nurturing and building up and enjoying our children. There is nothing in our schedules—not the pressure of business nor community commitments nor church commitments—that is more urgent and more important than the relationships we are building with our children.

Forgiven, Accepted, Affirmed

Let's take another look at Colossians 3:21—"Fathers, do not embitter your children, or they will become discouraged." I think there's a lot of meaning bound up in that one word *discouraged*. The apostle Paul is giving us profound advice here, telling us how to raise up children who are courageous enough to stand alone against peer pressure, against the sneers and persecution and abuse that Christian young people must face when they take a public stand for Jesus Christ. He's telling us how to raise children with a sound, healthy sense of self-esteem and self-worth. He's telling us how to raise children who feel forgiven, accepted, and affirmed.

Low self-esteem always begins in childhood, and it often begins in the home, in the way we relate to our children. They seek approval and affirmation and a sense that they are *pleasing* to their parents from the very earliest age.

Children who have become discouraged, who struggle with low self-esteem, with a broken sense of self-worth, are much more likely to give in to peer pressure, to engage in sinful, harmful, and self-destructive acts in order to please their friends. A child who is secure in the knowledge that he is accepted and forgiven and loved within his family stands much less danger of fearing rejection from others outside his family. When it comes time to make a moral choice in front of his friends, the child who is affirmed by his parents will be able to make his choice without worrying, "What will the rest of the kids think of me if I don't go along with this?" He'll have the inner strength, peace, and self-assurance to stand alone for what is right, and for Jesus Christ.

But how do we go about affirming our children?

It might be helpful to remember that there's an important distinction between *appreciation* and *affirmation*. We appreciate what a person *does*, but we affirm who a person *is*. Appreciation comes and goes because it is usually related to something a person accomplishes. You may appreciate it when your child keeps his room clean or does his chores well or gets good grades in school and accomplishes a medal-winning athletic feat in school sports.

But you can and should *affirm* your child when he's down, when he's failed, when he's made a mistake, when he's disobeyed, when he's sinned, when he's hurting, when he feels useless or misunderstood. We appreciate what a person *does*, but we affirm who a person *is*. Affirmation is forgiveness, encouragement, consolation, inspiration, acceptance, and unconditional love. Affirmation is saying to your child—verbally, through touching, through a smile and eye contact, and through quiet times of friendship and just being together—"You're my child and I love you, and I will always love you, no matter what you do."

Indeed, the ability to love, affirm, accept, and forgive others is passed from generation to generation. Children pick it up from their parents as they become the recipients of their mothers' and fathers' words and deeds of forgiveness, delight, affirmation, and encouragement. Tragically, too many homes in America—including too many *Christian* homes today—tend to be far more negative than positive, far more critical than affirming.

Your family doesn't have to be like that.

I recently heard Chuck Swindoll, on his nationally syndicated radio Bible program, tell the story of one of his classmates in seminary, a young man we'll call Tom. Tom was a bright, outgoing, gregarious, gifted young man, well-liked by his peers. This wouldn't be unusual at all, except for one thing: Tom had a large red birthmark that ran from one eye, down his face, across his mouth, down his neck, to his chest.

One day after they had become very good and close friends, Chuck asked Tom, "How did you overcome the emotional pain of your birthmark?"

"Oh," he answered quickly, "it's because of my dad. You see, he always told me, right from the time I was able to understand, 'Son, *this*' "—and he pointed along the length of his birthmark—" 'this is where an angel kissed you, because he wanted to mark you out just for your dad. You're very special to me, and whenever we're in a group of people, I always know right away where you are, and that you're mine.' My dad told me that so many times that I even began to feel sorry for all my friends who didn't have a birthmark."

Our kids have some tough times ahead. As they're growing and learning and trying and sometimes failing, they will get roughed up a bit, scarred a bit, marked by sins and disappointments and defeats. They need to be built up and freely forgiven.

They need to be encouraged to go on, to become all they can be for the glory of God. They need to be given the affirmation and self-assurance that will enable them to stand boldly and firmly against peer pressure, temptation, frustration, and discouragement. They need to hear, again and again and again, "I'm on your side, not on your back."

"Do not embitter your children, or they will become discouraged." May God give us an expanded, exalted vision of the gift He gave us when he entrusted these tender, pliable young lives to our care. And may we take seriously the responsibility and the privilege we have to give these precious children our time, to affirm them when they fail, to ask their forgiveness when we fail, to lead them and guide them into a strong and confident sense of self-worth and self-esteem—

And to *enjoy* them.

12

Anger and Forgiveness

Mary was a Christian woman well-known for her smiling, easygoing disposition. Mary *never* got angry.

One day in the course of a minor argument with a neighbor woman over some inconsequential issue, "easygoing Mary" suddenly became vehemently angry. She picked up a bottle of caustic cleaning fluid and hurled the contents into her neighbor's face. That neighbor woman is today blinded and scarred for life.

Why did this happen?

Later this Christian woman, with the help of Christian counseling, came to understand that her tragic behavior toward her neighbor was the result of years and years of repressed anger. Throughout her life she had often been upset and hurt. She had inwardly harbored angry feelings toward others in her church and her neighborhood, but she had been taught since childhood that it was wrong and unchristian to express anger. So she had denied and buried her anger, pressing it deep inside, where it grew unseen like a destructive malignancy. When it finally and inevitably surfaced, a woman was left maimed and disfigured.

Repression or Ventilation?

Anger is an inescapable part of life. Christians in the 1980s are caught between two opposing views of how to deal with anger: 1) a traditional view, that all anger is sin and should be repressed, buried, submerged; or 2) the prevailing cultural view of the 1980s, that anger is a tangible mass of unhealthy emotions that must be released, gotten out of your system and off your chest.

Carol Tavris in her book *Anger: The Misunderstood Emotion* assails the view that expressing anger is crucial to health and happiness as "one of today's most accepted myths of popular psychology." She convincingly asserts her view that the unrestrained expression of anger—screaming at someone, telling someone off, breaking something—tends to *complicate*, not reduce, our frustrations, and threatens further harm to relationships that may already be in a fragile condition. "Letting off steam," she writes, "is a wonderful metaphor and seems to capture exactly how angry outbursts work—but people are not teapots. . . . Letting off steam can make the atmosphere very hot and humid."[76]

Tavris calls the prevailing practice of aggressively venting our anger "ventilationism," and concludes that this form of behavior actually *stimulates* rather than assuages our hostility and anxiety. This in turn raises the blood pressure and adrenaline levels, and the result is greater physical stress and risk to health. Tavris cites study after study to confirm these conclusions, including these two:

> Murray Straus, a sociologist in the field of family violence, finds that couples who yell at each other do not thereafter feel less angry but more angry. Verbal aggression and physical aggression were highly correlated in his studies, which means it is a small step from bitter

accusations to slaps.

Leonard Berkowitz [a research psychologist at the University of Wisconsin], who has studied the social causes of aggression for many years, likewise finds that ventilation-by-yelling has no effect on the reduction of anger. "Telling someone we hate him supposedly will purge pent-up aggressive inclinations and will 'clear the air,' " he observed. "Frequently, however, when we tell someone off, we stimulate ourselves to continued or even stronger aggression."[77]

The Bible has a great deal to say about anger, and in recent years we have begun to see that psychological and medical research are beginning to confirm what the Bible has been saying all along.

The Anger of God Versus the Anger of Man

The Old Testament alone contains over 450 occurrences of the Hebrew word for anger. Indeed, the majority of these passages refer to the anger of God. It's important, however, to understand the *nature* of God's character, even in those times when He became angry.

God never held grudges against His people, no matter how far they strayed from His love and His law. Rather, the prophet Nehemiah was able to praise God because He stood by the Israelites, loving them unconditionally even when they forsook Him and committed awful blasphemies. "You are a forgiving God," says Nehemiah 9:17, "gracious and compassionate, slow to anger and abounding in love."[78] Though sojourners in an unforgiving world, the children of Israel served a forgiving, compassionate God—the same God of forgiveness we serve today.

In the New Testament, James encourages us to build into our character the same qualities Nehemiah depicts in God's character: "Everyone should be quick to listen, slow to speak and slow to become angry," James says. And then he draws a clear distinction between God's anger and ours: "For man's anger does not bring about the righteous life that God desires."[79]

Times of frustration and provocation are *inevitable* in life. We all know that. Anger is a fact of life, and indeed a fact of the *Christian life*. We may well wonder, Is there a proper place in the church for the expression of anger? Is it God's will that we remove feelings of anger from our lives? Or does He offer in His Word a way to express love, acceptance, and forgiveness even *during* times of anger?

These are the central questions that the follower of Jesus Christ must answer about anger and forgiveness. These are the questions we will attempt to squarely face.

What Does the Bible Say?

The Old Testament is filled with instruction about anger. Solomon, that great man of godly wisdom, has this to say: "A gentle answer turns away wrath, but a harsh word stirs up anger."[80] "Do not be quickly provoked in your spirit, for anger resides in the lap of fools."[81]

The New Testament is also filled with admonitions about anger.[82] Implicit throughout these admonitions is the basic assumption that we will have natural feelings of anger—that anger, even in the life of the Christian, is to be expected. In Ephesians 4:26 the apostle Paul gives us a twofold piece of advice, beginning with a quote from Psalm 4:4: "In your anger do not sin." Then he concludes in his own words, "Do not let the sun go down while you are still angry."

Over the years there has been some confusion over this verse because some versions translate those first words of Ephesians 4:26 something like "Be angry, and sin not." Note that this is *not* a command that we are to build anger into our character; rather, this is simply Paul's acknowledgment that we will sometimes have feelings of anger. The New International Version makes this clear: "In your anger do not sin."

The rest of that verse advises, "Do not let the sun go down while you are still angry." Don't let your natural feelings of anger turn into sin; don't let too much time go by without positively *resolving* those feelings of anger. Throughout the Scriptures there is an implicit acknowledgment that all of us will have angry feelings toward other people at times. How we choose to respond to those natural feelings of anger will determine whether we have acted sinfully or righteously.

Jesus, Our Example

God's goal for our lives, according to Romans 8:29, is that we be conformed into the image, the likeness, the character of His Son, Jesus Christ. There are areas of our lives which the Lord wants to reshape into conformity with His own perfect character—areas we are blind to until they are illuminated for us. So we need to ask ourselves, "Is it possible that I have a problem with unresolved anger but am unaware of it? How can I allow God to reshape those areas into mature, Christlike character?"

Let me suggest a simple test for hidden anger. Just review your behavior during the past week toward other people, toward situations of stress and frustration, toward your family, toward other drivers on the road, toward your co-workers and fellow Christians. Examine your heart honestly before God.

Did you this past week give way to sudden outbursts of rage? Have you spent time secretly dwelling on malicious thoughts toward others? Have you used abusive language in a frustrating circumstance or with a difficult person? Have you called anyone a contemptuous name, either in your thoughts or aloud? Do you feel bitter toward someone in your family, church, or business? Have you been in an argument with someone and made no attempt to reconcile with him or her? If so, then you have areas of anger in your life that need to be brought under the control of the Holy Spirit.

If Christlikeness is our goal, then Jesus is our Model. What are we to learn about anger and forgiveness from His teaching and His example?

Jesus took the subject of anger very seriously. In the Sermon on the Mount He said, "You have heard that it was said to the people long ago, 'Do not murder, and anyone who murders will be subject to judgment.' But I tell you that anyone who is angry with his brother will be subject to judgment. Again, anyone who says to his brother, 'Raca,' [an angry contemptuous Aramaic epithet], is answerable to the Sanhedrin. But anyone who says, 'You fool!' will be in danger of the fire of hell."[83]

Jesus places the expression of anger on the same plane as murder. When we call another person contemptuous names, whether openly or in our own thoughts, or treat others with derision or scorn, we have committed sin.

But Jesus, like Paul, recognizes that moments of provocation are inevitable in life, and He shows us what our response should be when our anger is provoked: We must seek reconciliation and forgiveness with the person who has angered us. "First go and be reconciled to your brother; then come and offer your gift."[84] If we are unwilling to forgive one another and deal with our anger positively and constructively, then our religious acts mean nothing.

There were times of provocation and anger in the life of Jesus. We know, for example, that He was angry with the Pharisees when He pronounced seven woes upon them, comparing them to burial crypts filled with corruption. We know that the hardness of their proud religious hearts angered Him. But the most well-known instance of Jesus' anger is found in John 2:13-17, when He angrily and violently drove the merchants and corrupt moneychangers from the Jerusalem temple.

The cleansing of the temple is an event in Christ's life that's hard for some of us to grasp. We may ask, "Didn't Jesus simply lose His temper when He drove out the moneychangers? If we are to be imitators of Christ, shouldn't we also imitate Him by openly expressing any anger we feel?"

Notice the target of Jesus' anger: He was angry with the religious leaders, merchants, and profiteers who had turned a holy place of worship into a profane and shameful carnival. So He made a whip of cords and drove the sellers out of the temple, scattered the coins of the moneychangers, and overturned their tables.

Why? Because He was angry with *injustice and political corruption disguised as religion*. His anger was *not* ignited by zeal for His own interests, His own ego, or for any of the other petty, selfish concerns that so easily unleash the anger in us. Rather, John 2:17 tells us that His zeal was *for His Father's house*.

Look at James 1:19,20. "Be quick to listen, slow to speak and slow to become angry, for man's anger does not bring about the righteous life that God desires." The New American Standard Bible translates this, "The anger of man does not achieve the righteousness of God." What Jesus was doing in John 2 was *exercising the anger of God to achieve the righteousness of God.* But James reminds us that the expression of *human* anger can *never* achieve the righteousness of God.

Tender Toughness

Contrary to the culturally ingrained stereotype of Christ—the effeminate-seeming Christ of religious paintings and stained glass—the real, historical, flesh-and-blood Jesus Christ of the Gospels was a bold, authoritative, magnetic man. He attracted huge crowds and confronted corrupt religious officials to the point that they reacted with bloodthirsty vengeance. I'm convinced that one of the most attractive qualities of Jesus' personality was that perfect integration of tenderness and toughness in His life.

People were attracted to Christ because He spoke boldly, with authority, with resounding courage, and yet He was also gentle with those whose lives He touched. To be Christlike in this area of our lives is to exhibit *tender toughness* in all our dealings. Christ is our example in His forgiveness, in His obedience, in His humility, in His gentleness, in His prayerfulness, in His boldness, in His courage, in His toughness against sin, and in His tenderness with sinners.

It's right for us to grieve over the things that break the heart of God, and to be angry at the things that anger God. It's right for us to be angry at injustice. It's right for us to be so angry at the evils of hunger and poverty that we are compelled to take action to help those in need. It's right for us to loathe sin and immorality and malice, especially when we discover these sins in our own hearts. But we are *never* justified in directing our anger toward other people, causing injury to others, breaking relationships with others, or failing to immediately forgive others, especially others in our family of faith, the church.

We need to build forgiving, Christlike tender toughness into our lives. We need to stand for the way Jesus Christ related to people. We need to understand that He was tough on sin but tender, accepting, and forgiving toward sinners, even those who were lost in sin, even those who betrayed Him.

I know many tender Christians—warm, emotional, sensitive people whose gentleness enables them to express compassion and affirmation to others. I also know many Christians whom I admire for their toughness, because they stand so faithfully for Jesus Christ, with tough determination, tough integrity, tough directness in their words and their life. In a world of compromise, they refuse to compromise. Their words have congruence with their character.

The problem in the church today is that tender Christians generally need to become a little more tough, and tough Christians generally need to become a little more tender. This is a vital balance to find if we are really going to be conformed into the image of Christ. If we fail to find that balance, we will ultimately settle toward one extreme or the other, and in the end we will have two kinds of Christians in the church: the tender Christians who have softened into mere weak sentimentalists, and the tough Christians who have hardened into harsh, unyielding Pharisees.

Understand that Christlike tenderness is not weakness. Rather, it's a special kind of strength under control. It's the ability to clearly, boldly state one's convictions, even in the face of great opposition, even in the face of open hostility, yet with inner peace and outward kindness. The quality of Christlike tender-toughness enables us to face the anger of other people with calm, unconditional love and forgiveness. The Christian who evinces tender toughness seeks only to help, not hurt; to heal, not cripple;

to forgive and reconcile, not exact revenge.

God's Perspective on Anger

We need to gain God's perspective for our times of anger and annoyance. We need to understand that feelings of anger are initially neither good nor bad—they are just feelings. The initial provocation we feel in a moment of conflict or frustration is not sin. It is *temptation*. It is then *our choice* whether we will overrule that provocation, that temptation, or whether it will rule over us, festering into rage, malice, blasphemy, slander, or hate.

Those initial *feelings* of anger are simply a part of our humanity, and they remain with us even after our conversion to Christ. We do a great disservice to people when we make them feel guilty because of emotions that are normal and natural, and not at all sinful.

We also need to grasp the biblical fact that it is unwholesome and sinful for us to stay angry for a long period. Don't let the sun go down on your anger; resolve it today. Keep short accounts with people who have provoked you. When we are careful not to bottle up and repress anger inside us, we improve the health not only of our bodies, but also the health of our relationships toward God and other people.

We need to take personal ownership of our anger. We need to stop blaming our anger on others. We need to stop saying, "You make me angry!" We need to start acknowledging that, no matter who or what provokes the anger within us, our *response* is our *responsibility*. In his book *The Meaning and Mystery of Being Human*, Bruce Larson writes, "No one can make you angry. You choose to allow someone to make you angry. You are not someone else's victim."

We have to begin directing our anger toward the problem, not the person. Instead of shouting, "You're making me mad!" we need to be able to sincerely say, "I feel angry about the problem between us. You and I as Christians, as two people who are committed to each other, need to form a partnership together *against* the anger, *against* the problem. Together we can focus on the problem until it is resolved. Then we can get on with the business of loving each other.''

The difficulty with anger is that we often lose our sense of God's priorities. Our first priority in any conflict with a loved one, with another Christian, must always be the *relationship*. All other issues, including the issues we are arguing about, are secondary.

The Third Option

There are two extreme views in our culture today regarding anger and how to deal with it: 1) all anger should be *repressed*; and 2) all anger should be *expressed*. I submit, however, that there is a *third option*, an option for responding to anger that is not only thoroughly biblical, but more practical and more healthy then either repression or unrestrained expression. I believe that the Word of God affirms this healthy, humble, loving, gentle, righteous, forgiving way of dealing with anger: Our anger should be *confessed*.

Sometimes confession of anger should occur between you and the person you are struggling with. At other times you may only be able to confess your anger to God and talk it through with Him. I'm suggesting something that I've found to be rarely mentioned in all the discussions and books I've heard or seen on anger: the central role of *prayer*, of a sharing, open relationship with Christ.

Through prayer we have complete access to God. We can go to Him, acknowledging our true feelings. Then, when it's appropriate, we can go to that brother or sister who has provoked us and we can lovingly, gently, humbly confess and discuss our feelings so we can find reconciliation.

The spirit in which we confess our anger is so important, and that spirit of gentleness and unconditional love doesn't arise naturally in our sinful nature. It comes to us *supernaturally*, as we go to God in prayer and as we continue, moment by moment, to *rely on God*, silently asking Him to live out His love and gentleness in us, even while we are going through the hard process of talking to the one who has provoked our anger.

If someone had asked me a few years ago, "Is there a place for anger in the church?," I would have unhesitatingly answered no. When I entered the ministry, almost 20 years ago, my dream and my goal before God was that He would use me as a catalyst to help people love, accept, and forgive each other. No matter how much I fail in that or how inadequate I am, that is still my goal today. Yet through my early ministry I was unable to reconcile the natural, inevitable occurrence of anger in my life (and the lives of other Christians) to my desire to see people love one another.

In recent years, however, I have come to realize that it is *in the midst of struggle* and the inevitable feelings of anger on various sides that our bond of fellowship in Jesus Christ is proved, that our unconditional love for one another is displayed. I've found that we can communicate *through* the process of differing with each other that our greatest concern is our love relationship with Christ and with each other.

There is so much that God wants to teach us—things He can only teach us through a process of struggle, differing opinions, and conflict. How open are you to God, and to what He is trying to teach you through your own feelings of anger, and through the anger and opposition of other people? How open are you to finding that balance of tender toughness that will bring honor to God and will conform you into the very image of Jesus Christ?

Anger Toward God

Confession is also vital in those difficult times when our anger is directed not toward another person, but toward God. Yes, if we are honest, we must confess that there are times when we angrily ask God, "Why? Why did You allow this to happen? Are You in control or aren't You?" And God understands when you feel that way. The channel is open. Tell Him honestly how you feel.

Let me tell you two stories about two different families. Both were visited by tragedy and both experienced anger toward God. Yet in these stories we see two families exhibiting two very different responses to tragedy and to their anger toward God.

John was a vital, enthusiastic, energetic young Christian, active in high school sports and in his church's youth group. The son of Christian parents, John had accepted Christ into his life at a very early age. He was well-known for his outgoing, winsome way of living his faith on the athletic field, on campus, and at home.

Suddenly, at the age of 17, John's life was ended by a senseless accident. At his funeral, the church was filled with people who loved John and his family. The minister could not get through the service without tears, nor could many of the other friends and well-wishers who had come to pay last respects to a young man who had died too soon. Even though there was a strong note of triumph in the eulogy because John had known a personal relationship with Jesus Christ, and even though there was a certainty that John was at peace with the Lord, the sorrow of that church was deep, and there were few dry eyes anywhere in that sanctuary.

John's family, however, shed no tears. They expressed no grief. Though they must have had many searching questions about the numbing pointlessness of their son's death at such an early age, they displayed no questioning, no anger. Many people who attended that funeral commented on the courage of this family, on their strength, on their acceptance of God's permissive will.

The next Sunday they were at church in their accustomed pew. And Sunday after Sunday, week after week, they maintained the same stiff-upper-lip facade. Gradually people began to realize that the friendliness, the warmth, the fun, the joy of living that had once characterized John's family was now gone. What people had originally taken for courage, strength, and acceptance of God's will soon became evident as a kind of cold, joyless stoicism. Weeks turned into months, and then into years, and no joy ever returned to this family's life.

Why?

Ann Kiemel, in her cassette tape message called *Hi, I'm Ann!*, tells a similarly tragic story, but with a much different ending. On one of her trips to a speaking engagement, Ann was picked up at the airport by a married couple, friends she hadn't seen since college. In their arms they carried Paula, their little girl, who had braces on her legs, the result of cerebral palsy. As they were getting into the car, Paula climbed into Ann's lap and said, "Ann, I have a new baby brother."

Seeing no baby, Ann asked, "Where is he?"

Paula's mother turned around from the front seat and said, "Ann, Paula doesn't understand. God did give us a little baby boy a few months ago, but he only lived for a few weeks."

She went on to explain that after their baby died, they became angry with God. They asked Him, "*Why* did this happen? *Why* was this baby born perfect and healthy and normal, only to die a few weeks later from a sudden and unexpected respiratory infection? *Why* was he snatched from us so suddenly?"

"And Ann," she concluded, "we still don't have all the answers, but we're working it through. Our anger and our pain has gradually been replaced by His peace. And even though we don't understand why He took our baby away, we do understand that He's given us a ministry to other parents who have lost little babies. And He's given us a ministry to other parents of children with cerebral palsy, like Paula. We're reaching scores of people for Christ who could never have been reached otherwise, and we're thankful to God for that."

Two couples, both of whom lost children, and two entirely different responses: one of stoic repression of anger, the other of honest confession of anger and grief to the Lord; one of cold, stony denial of grief, the other of openness and healing.

God is willing to accept whatever feelings we have, even our anger. He understands, He loves us, and He accepts us without conditions.

The way to a healthy response to our feelings of anger—either anger toward others or toward God—lies *not* in repressing and burying our feelings. It lies in confessing them, in giving open and constructive expression to those feelings through prayer and through words and deeds of love, forgiveness, and reconciliation. Through confession, it is possible to be angry, yet without sin.

13

Defamation of Character

Defamation of character: She was new to the church, a pretty, outgoing, friendly high school girl. She made friends quickly, and became active in the church youth group. Soon, however, rumors about her began to surface. It was reputed that she had loose morals, and that she had become pregnant and had an abortion before joining the church. Some of her new friends began to withdraw from her; others treated her with condescension; others were uneasy in her presence. Through it all, no one had he courage to confront her directly about these stories.

Late in the year it was discovered that the rumors were in fact completely false. The person who had begun the rumor had this girl confused with someone else—but the damage had been done. Her reputation had been tainted by a rumor, and the damage could never be fully undone.

Defamation of character: Shortly before we moved to California from Minneapolis, I received several reports about two well-known Christian leaders on the West Coast, both friends of mine, both men who were famous for their emphasis on family relations and reconciliation. According to these rumors, both of these men had gone through the painful upheaval of divorce, and their ministries had been shattered as a result.

On moving to the West Coast, I found that these rumors were totally false. But the lies told about these men had spread at least as far as the Midwest, and probably far beyond, so that the credibility of these excellent, caring men of God was now called into question, and their reputations and those of their families were damaged.

Defamation of character: A young woman was in my office sharing with me her disillusionment over her college prayer group. "At the beginning of our prayer time, we always share requests for prayer," she said. "Inevitably there will be three or four girls who, when they share their requests, will go on to give long, detailed reports about the sordid activities of some friend of theirs who is involved in some sin, or making some mistake. Instead of just saying, 'Ann or Susan needs God's help in such-and-such an area,' these girls seem to delight in spilling all the gory details before the group." Even in the midst of prayer and Christian fellowship—defamation of character.

Defamation of character: A high school student sat in my office, asking my advice about a crisis in his life. He had a major decision to make, and the consequences of that decision would unquestionably affect his future for many years to come.

"Have you talked this decision over with your folks?" I asked.

"Are you kidding, Ron?" he said with a vehemence that surprised me. "I can't talk to Mom about a thing like this! She tells everybody everything! This isn't the kind of thing I want blabbed around Ladies' Prayer Fellowship and the Bridge Club. I can't share *anything* with my folks."

Defamation of character: Something like this has happened to me scores of times, in every church I've ever worked in: Mr. Jones, a layman in the church, takes me aside and says, "I think there's something you ought to know about Mr. Smith. You see, he's one person you never want to work in a leadership role. He's defensive. His children are rebellious. He's weak, and he lacks leadership qualities."

But I decide to set aside Mr. Jones' advice, and I begin to work with Mr. Smith, asking him to take on a given responsibility in the church. I watch Mr. Smith's work and begin to see growing evidence of previously untapped spiritual gifts and abilities in his personality. True, at times he can be defensive (as we all are at times). And true, his children do test their limits (as all children do from time to time); but I also notice that the Smith children are well-disciplined and well-loved. Occasionally—rarely—Mr. Smith even fails in some task (as everyone eventually will if he commits himself to such a role).

But overall Mr. Smith turns out to be a valuable, capable, gifted layman. The tragedy is that for years he has been kept from discovering and exercising his gifts because other laymen had spread prejudice about him.

Accuracy Versus Truth

There is one sin, one act of unforgiveness that causes incalculably more damage to relationships, to homes, and to churches than almost any other sin, and yet we almost universally excuse and laugh off this vicious sin as an essentially harmless human foible.

This sin is pervasive, it is destructive, it is condemned in the strongest terms throughout the Old and New Testament. This sin breaks friendships and thwarts efforts to bring reconciliation. It is the centerpiece of Satan's strategy for *dividing and conquering* the church.

Part self-righteous pride, part malice, part grudge-bearing, part envy, part bitterness, this sin combines the worst components of many sins to achieve their most cruel and deadly effect in the lives of those around us. Thus it is *diametrically opposed* to Christlike forgiveness.

It is the forgotten sin.

The Bible calls it *spreading an evil report*. Or *gossip*. Or *slander*. Or *spreading rumors*. Or *breaking a confidence*. The legal term is *defamation of character*.

At one time or another this sin touches us all. Some of us are guilty of spreading rumors about others, and need to experience the conviction of the Holy Spirit in this area of our lives. Other of us are victims of this sin, and need to receive the encouragement and comfort of God for our trial.

Spreading a word of gossip may simply involve the act of telling some third party a *lie* about someone else. But usually our gossiping is more sophisticated than that. We may tell a distorted or incomplete version of the accurate facts about someone. Or we may simply give our subjective opinion of another person's character or intentions or actions.

Deadliest of all, we may even tell the accurate, complete facts about someone else, but do so from a malicious motive, turning "truth" into a skewer upon which we impale others for our own prideful, self-righteous satisfaction. Jesus said, "The truth will set you free."[85] But when we use the truth maliciously, in order to hurt and enslave others, or to feed our own pride, then the truth ceases to be the truth anymore. Out of our sinful, prideful motives, we can pervert the truth into something more deadly and destructive than any lie.

The film *Absence of Malice* depicts a reporter who recklessly prints what she believes to be the truth. In the process she brings enormous harm to several innocent people and discredit to herself as a reporter. By the end of the film she is remorseful and wiser, but the damage can't be undone. She is asked by another reporter to tell her story, which is to appear in the paper as a front-page retraction. Partway through her story the other reporter interrupts and asks, "Is that the *truth*?" And she replies, "No—but it's *accurate*." This reporter had learned a hard lesson that we all need to learn: the difference between what is *accurate* and what is *true*.

It may be accurate to say, "John is so unfriendly, so cold, so withdrawn. I don't even like to be around him." But the *truth* may be that John is struggling with a broken self-image, that he lacks self-confidence, that he's wounded in spirit, and that if he's ever going to find healing, people are going to have to reach out to him. The *truth* is that people would rather talk about John and criticize him than help him become whole.

It may be accurate to say, "Mary's just gone through a messy divorce. I hear from reliable sources that she attempted suicide right after the divorce, and that she's seeing a psychiatrist now." But the *truth* may be that she tried for five years to keep her marriage together, that her husband was repeatedly unfaithful to her, then abused her and finally tossed her aside. Indeed, the deepest, most awful truth may be that her despair over the incessant prying and gossiping about her personal tragedy has driven her toward suicide and forced her into psychoanalysis.

It may be accurate to say, "Pastor Brown's sermons never relate to me. I think he's the dullest, driest pastor this church has ever had!" But the *truth* may be that his sermons are a source of real teaching and blessing to the majority of people in the church; that those who criticize him have closed their hearts and minds to him, and to what God would desperately like to teach them through his ministry; that they have never simply prayed and asked God to speak to them through his messages.

The facts that we are relating to various third parties may be "accurate," but our motives are sinful, our report is evil, and the gulf between what is *accurate* and what is *true* is abysmally vast.

Our Perspective or God's?

Gossip and forgiveness are mutually exclusive acts. Forgiveness is the willful, conscious, active process of erasing and forgetting a sin or a flaw or a wrong. Gossip is the willful, conscious, active process of perpetuating and widening and deepening the memory of a sin, a flaw, or a wrong.

It is recorded that Clara Barton, the pioneer founder of the American Red Cross, was once reminded by a co-worker of a malicious act that someone had committed against her a long time before. Though this act had been a terrible, wounding injustice, she acted as though she had no memory of the event.

"Don't you remember what that person did to you, and how much you were hurt by it?" her co-worker asked in disbelief.

"No," she replied with gentle finality. "I distinctly remember forgetting it."

So should our forgiving be: active, aggressive, determined *forgetfulness* of wrongs suffered. Tragically, our response to a wrong suffered is all too often not one of forgiveness, but of determinedly keeping the memory alive. We replay the memory over and over in our own minds, and we vengefully play back the details for anyone else who will listen. In a spirit of revenge and unforgiveness, we gossip, we slander, we spread an evil report.

Why do we enjoy talking about other people—about their problems, sins, and defeats? Why are we fascinated to hear gossip about others? I believe it's because we fail to understand what the Bible really says about gossip. We lack God's perspective on this sin.

If we are honest with ourselves, we have to admit that our perspective on gossip is shaped more by our culture than by the Word of God. In America in the 1980s, gossip is an *industry*: National magazines and television talk shows sell unrelenting streams of rumor and scandal. In a culture that places a premium on "pulling your own strings" and "looking out for number one," gossip is a way to get even, to manipulate events, to put people in their place. Gossip and slander are an ever-present part of office intrigues and business power-plays.

But God's view of gossip and slander is strict and unequivocal. Not only is this sin prohibited by the Ninth Commandment,[86] but it is one of many unforgiving acts listed throughout the New Testament. "I am afraid that when I come...there may be quarreling, jealousy, outbursts of anger, factions, slander, gossip, arrogance and disorder."[87] "Get rid of all bitterness, rage and anger, brawling and slander, along with every form of malice."[88]

The world we live in takes gossip for granted, laughs it off, and excuses it. *God's Word condemns it as sin.* We need to have *God's* perspective on the sin of gossip, not the perspective of the unforgiving world around us.

A Spiritual Virus

As a virus infects and destroys a human body, so defamation of character infects and destroys the body of Christ, the church. There is a step-by-step process that takes place when the human body contracts a viral infection; the infection of a church by the virus of gossip and slander proceeds by a similar set of steps.

Step 1: Exposure. Often we are unaware that we are surrounded by contagion, by a disease-causing virus. Thus we fail to take precautions against infection—precautions such as distancing ourselves from the carrier of the infection. Thus we become *exposed* to a virus.

Similarly, the spiritual contagion of gossip surrounds us, yet we are often unaware of the danger it poses. So we permit ourselves to hear a rumor, and we create an environment that is conducive for the spiritual virus of gossip to thrive around us. We become *exposed.*

Step 2: Contamination. Like a virus, the defaming report we've heard enters our thinking. The reputation and character of the person we've heard about becomes colored in our minds. Whether the rumor is accurate, semi-accurate, or a total lie, we will be unable to think of that person in the same way again. We may be unable to even see that person without thinking of the gossip we've heard. Our relationship with that person has become contaminated, and our own spirit has become defiled.

Part of the perverse "pleasure" of listening to gossip is that it inflates our *pride*, and pride is one of the most insidious, destructive sins that threaten us. Like most sins and character flaws, pride is more easily detected in other people than in ourselves. Thus we need to continually, thoroughly search ourselves, while asking God to enlighten us to the areas of sinful pride that lie hidden within us.

Some of us are eager to receive rumors because we take pride in knowing about everything that's going on around us. We enjoy having a reputation for being knowledgeable, for always having "the scoop." The Bible says, "Knowledge puffs up, but love builds up."[89] We need to seek love, not the latest news on "who did what to whom."

Some of us are eager to hear gossip because it enables us to feel superior to the victim of the tale. If someone tells us about someone else's scandal or tragedy or character flaws, then we have an opportunity to smugly "sympathize" over the woes or faults of "poor Joe" or "poor Jane." What self-deception in the sin of pride! "I hate pride and arrogance, evil behavior and perverse speech," says the Lord in Proverbs 8:13. "The pride of your heart has deceived you," is the sober warning of Obadiah 1:3.

If we receive an evil report about another person, then in our pride we deceive and contaminate and defile ourselves. But if we are humble, confessing our sins to God, refusing to listen to the worst tales and opinions about our neighbors, then we will be exalted in the eyes of God.

Step 3: Infection. After an organism becomes contaminated by a virus, the next step is for it to become *infected*; the bodily functions become inhibited, diseased. So it is with the human spirit and the virus of gossip.

We become infected as we begin to *believe* an evil report. Think back on a recent conversation you had in which you've heard someone gossiped about. That should be fairly easy, since rumors circulate through most churches, families, offices, clubs, and friendships like flames through dry grass. As you think back on that conversation, ask yourself these questions:

1) Do you believe the evil report you heard?
2) Has your opinion of the person you heard about been diminished or negatively colored? Do you now think less of that person?
3) When you are with the person you heard about, do you now begin to interpret things he says and does as supporting evidence for the rumor you heard?
4) Have you begun to distance yourself from that person?
5) Most importantly, have you begun to pass that rumor

on to other people?

If you have to honestly answer yes to any of the first four questions, then you have become infected by an evil report. And if you have to answer yes to question 5, then you are spreading that infection and becoming an accessory to Satan's strategy for multiplying division in the church.

As we become infected by gossip, our function in the body of Christ gradually becomes unhealthy and unbiblical. Our *opinions* of others become more important than our *love and forgiveness* toward them. We become critical fault-finders rather than agents of unity and reconciliation.

Step 4: Destruction. As the virus ultimately destroys the organism it has infected, so gossip eventually kills our spiritual organism. As individuals, we become unteachable, hardened of heart, unforgiving, equipped only to spread the poison of gossip to other people. As a church, we become mistrustful, vengeful, and fragmented. Once-healthy ministries fall prey to suspicion and innuendo. The vital functions of a church cease, and the gospel of God's wholeness and forgiveness is brought down in shame and disgrace.

The symptoms of the destructive effect of slander and gossip are these: 1) We develop bitterness toward the person who has been gossiped about, even when they've done nothing to hurt us personally; 2) we set ourselves up as judge in matters where God alone is Judge; 3) we begin to recruit people to our position; 4) we begin to seek out further gossip.

The Satanic Scheme: Divide and Conquer

Forgiveness is one of the most formidable weapons we have in the war against Satan. The scheme of Satan against the church is to *divide and conquer.* He seeks to divide the church by seducing us toward the sins of pride, suspicion, and gossip toward each other. By covering over the sins and flaws of our fellow Christians with a spirit of overflowing forgiveness, we defeat his scheme to render us ineffective in the service of God.

The apostle Paul tells us, "What I have forgiven...I have

forgiven in the sight of Christ for your sake, in order that Satan might not outwit us. For we are not unaware of his schemes."[90] Tragically, many of us are unaware of how Satan seeks to conquer and destroy the work of the body of Christ. Many of us are unaware of what the Bible teaches about spreading character defamation in the body of Christ. So in our ignorance—a sinful ignorance, caused by our failure to build the truth of God's Word into our lives—we surround ourselves with people who spread and receive gossip and slander.

A friend of mine, the pastor of a church in southern California, told me of a time he was preaching to his congregation on the subject of spiritual gifts. After his message, as he was greeting people at the door, one woman came up to him and thanked him for his sermon. "I want you to know that God has revealed to me what my spiritual gift is," she said in all seriousness. "I have the gift of criticism."

I think many of us in the church have taken upon ourselves the so-called "gift of criticism." We are using that hurtful "gift" to exalt ourselves in our own eyes, and to spread dissension and suspicion throughout the body of Christ. We do so because we are unaware that the New Testament teaches that this is the *central scheme* that Satan uses to divide us, to conquer us.

Why do we do this to each other in our families, in our jobs, in our churches? Why are we so eager to spread the spiritual disease of rumor and slander? I suspect there are two basic reasons.

First, we are insecure, and in our insecurity we project our own character flaws onto other people. If we are jealous by nature, very often the first thing we notice in the character of others is a trait of jealousy. If we ourselves are defensive by nature, then we are constantly finding ourselves rubbed the wrong way by the defensiveness of others. If we are dogmatic and unyielding in our opinions, then we will likely spread defaming reports to others about those we consider stubborn and inflexible toward our point of view.

A second motive—and an even more potent and self-deceptive motive—for spreading evil reports is that we often rationalize our gossip as being an attempt to "help" another person. I've seen this again and again as a pastor, as different people have come to me and said something like, "I'm really only saying this in the best interests of Bill—" and then they tell me their opinion of Bill's character or tell me of some problem area in Bill's life as they defame his character.

The spreading of a rumor or gossip cannot accomplish God's ultimate good. It simply cannot. I have never seen one verse in Scripture that supports the idea that we are to identify the faults and deficiencies and weaknesses of someone else, and to pass that information on to others as a way of "helping" someone. Rather, as Jesus said in Matthew 7:3,4, we should look first to the plank in our own eye before paying attention to the speck of sawdust in the eye of a brother.

Satan is seeking to blunt our effectiveness as Christians, to turn us against each other, to stir up war among us so we'll spend all our energies wounding each other, thereby becoming too weak to press the battle against *him*. He seduces us to spread the slanders and lies that bring spiritual leadership in the church into discredit. He causes Christians to close their hearts and minds toward one another, so that they withdraw from each other in distrust, grudge-bearing, and hatred. He multiplies and intensifies the conflicts between us, so that *factions* emerge, each faction focused on strategies to win the conflict and outflank the other side.

One particularly tragic consequence of these Christian civil wars is that the world rejects faith in Christ, concluding that people in the church are just as malicious, contentious, and vengeful as people in the world—so why become a Christian? At the same time, many Christians have become disillusioned or wounded by these church wars, and have left their churches or even their faith.

Detecting and Avoiding a Rumor

"Whoever spreads slander is a fool," says Proverbs 10:18. Perhaps you have been exposed to someone else's foolish slander.

Now you wish you had never heard it, but the damage is done. There's no way to unknow what you've already heard.

As with any other disease, the best treatment for the disease of slander is *prevention*. You can protect yourself against receiving gossip. You can detect the person who takes pleasure in spreading slander, and you can defend yourself against contamination by being *aware*.

You can know in advance that a word of gossip is headed your way because *the person carrying that gossip will always test your spirit*. And I assure you, if he sees any compatibility between your spirit and his, he will come back to you again and again with a defaming report.

He'll start by checking out your opinion. "What do you think about Bill?" he may say. Or, "How well do you know Mary?" Or he'll drop a subtle, delicately phrased, negative comment about someone, and watch your reaction. If you are at all receptive, he will go on to give you the details.

He may even manipulate you into asking a question. "Have you heard about Bill?" he may ask.

If you are not on your guard, if you are not careful as to what the Scriptures teach about receiving an evil report, you may respond, "No, what about Bill?" And he will proceed to contaminate your spirit with a defaming word about Bill.

Most beguiling of all, he may come to you asking for advice and counsel, saying, "I'm so concerned about Mary. What do you think we should do to help her?"

And you may reply, "Oh, I didn't know there was a problem with Mary."

And he'll say, "Really? I thought you knew. Well, I've said this much, so you might as well know the rest—so you can pray for her, of course . . ."

And then he will proceed to tell you all about Mary's problem.

Guard against the person who would seek to contaminate you with character defamation. Refuse to receive it, refuse to listen to it. Don't let it near you, and you won't have to worry about spreading the contagion to others.

Responding to a Gossip-Bearing Person

When you are exposed to someone who is spreading gossip, what should your response be? I've found that if we arm ourselves with *five simple questions*, we can be extremely effective at combating the rumor and slander that threatens our spirit and destroys our relationships.

1. *Why are you telling me?* Confront him with the question of his motives; encourage him to examine the reason for his actions. He has probably not thought through his own motivations.

2. *Where did you get your information?* The majority of rumors are based on secondhand, thirdhand, twelfthhand information. They almost invariably contain falsehood or omit crucial truths as a result of having been passed by the unreliable means of "the grapevine."

3. *Have you gone directly to the person you are telling me about?* This is perhaps the most crucial question of all. Jesus commands us to have the courage and integrity to deal with our differences face-to-face.[91] Rumor-spreading is almost always an act of cowardly unforgiveness. If someone complains to you about a wrong someone else did to him, you should tell him, "What you're telling me is really none of my business. You need to go to the one who has wronged you and courageously find reconciliation."

4. *Have you checked out all the facts?* If someone comes to you with a second or thirdhand tale, you should say, "You heard from so-called 'reliable sources' that Mary is involved in such-and-such activity. Have you gone to Mary and asked *her* about it? Perhaps she deserves a chance to defend herself against what may be just a misunderstanding or an outright lie. And if it's true, then Mary needs to be gently, lovingly corrected and restored, as it says in Galatians 6:1."

5. *Do you mind if I quote you?* It's amazing what impact *this* question has! I have yet to meet a courageous rumor-peddler, one who was willing to take personal responsibility for the slander he is spreading.

Galatians 6:1 makes our responsibility toward carriers of gossip clear: "Brothers, if someone is caught in a sin, you who are spiritual should restore him gently." That's not an option, that's our biblical duty. If someone comes to you with a rumor, you should confront him with what he is doing— directly and firmly, but in a spirit of gentleness. These five questions may be a good guide to helping that person deal with the sin of gossip in his own life.

God calls us to seek understanding where there is suspicion, and reconciliation where there is broken relationship. By having the courage to confront the sin of gossip, we can effectively defeat the scheme of Satan to divide and conquer the church.

Curing the Disease

"Consider what a great forest is set on fire by a small spark," says James 3:5,6; "the tongue also is a fire." Hebrews 12:15 warns, "See to it that no one misses the grace of God and that no bitter root grows up to cause trouble and defile many." Not few, but *many*. The firelike tongue of *one* person, spreading bitterness, spreading gossip, can cause *many* people to be defiled, wounded, broken, divided. The tongue of a gossip defiles not only his whole person, but the body of Christ as well. It's happened again and again in the history of the church.

I'm convinced that Satan is bringing more suffering to Christians by means of gossip and slander than by any other means. That is why I'm devoting so much space in this book to this one subject. The spiritual disease of gossip is like a cancer: It starts in a small and unnoticeable way, then spreads quickly and unseen, infiltrates the whole body, and kills the body slowly and agonizingly.

How can we be healed?

First, we need to cleanse our minds whenever we hear an evil report about a brother or sister in Christ. We have to set aside what we've heard, refuse to believe it. Even though our human tendency is to believe the worst, we must determine that our first presumption upon hearing gossip will be that it is *not* true.

Then we must begin to pray that God will give us genuine

and unconditional love for the person about whom gossip is being spread. We need to pray for that person, and to love him with the all-accepting love of Jesus Christ. We need to immerse ourselves in the Word of God, meditating daily in its pages, allowing its healing power to wash over us and renew our minds.

Our attitude must be that expressed by the apostle Paul: "Do not let any unwholesome talk come out of your mouths, but *only what is helpful for building others up* according to their needs, that it may benefit those who listen."[92] I guarantee that you will *never* impart the grace of God by defaming another Christian's character.

How will we know when we are healed?

We'll know we are healed when we *lose our urge* to hear and tell those things that are none of our business, when we *grieve* over a rumor we have heard, and when we have a genuine *love* for the person who is a victim of a rumor. May God so fill our hearts with His unconditional love, acceptance, and forgiveness, that we will have neither the time nor the inclination to speak anything of anyone—

Except words of grace and peace.

14

Definition of Character

When I was younger, still attending seminary, an elderly pastor came to me and asked me a question I've never forgotten. It was during the turbulent, activist decade of the 1960s and it was a turbulent, activist period of my own life as well. This wise old pastor was well aware of the shallowness and impetuousness that so often underlie the enthusiastic idealism of youth. So his question to me was "Ron, is the church a hospital or an army?"

I hardly had to consider the answer: "Oh, no question about that! The church is an *army*! We're battling injustice and immorality. We're in a cosmic struggle against the principalities and powers and world rulers of this dark age. We're an *army*."

He nodded thoughtfully, and said, "Well, then, Ron, let me

171

ask you this: What kind of army leaves its wounded deserted on the battlefield?''

Those words have never left me. The church *is* an army. But it is also a hospital. The great tragedy of the church, however, is that many of the wounded that we've left on the battlefield have been wounded by other members of their own army, their brothers and sisters in the body of Christ! They have been wounded by anger and malice and gossip and many other unforgiving acts.

How long will we go on decimating our own ranks? How long before we realize that the enemy is Satan, not our brother or sister in Christ?

Wounded Christian Soldiers

Most of us are familiar with the words to the first verse of the grand old hymn "Onward, Christian Soldiers." But I think there are very few of us who can recite the words to the *second* verse:

> Like a mighty army moves the Church of God;
> Brothers, we are treading where the saints have trod!
> We are not divided, all one body we!
> One in hope and doctrine, one in charity!

I can hardly sing those words without tears in my eyes—tears of sorrow over the hundreds of Christian civil wars that I have personally seen and often been caught in throughout my life. We should take it as an urgent, sober challenge to begin turning the words of that hymn into God's own truth for our lives, as we allow Him to transform us into soldiers of reconciliation in an army of unconditional love.

And yet I know that some who read these words are *wounded* Christian soldiers. Perhaps a loved one or a fellow Christian has wounded you through an act of unkindness or unforgiveness so painful that the hurt is as deep as grief itself. Sooner or later everyone becomes the victim of another's misunderstanding, gossip, grudge-bearing or bitterness. I have. I'm sure you have, too.

Perhaps someone has maliciously spread a false story about you; though you've done nothing wrong, your reputation has been damaged beyond hope of repair. Maybe someone withholds forgiveness and reconciliation from you, and cruelly rebuffs every attempt you make to restore that relationship. Or perhaps you have worked and struggled and suffered to achieve some dream, only to see the dream evaporate due to loss of employment, loss of health, or some mistake you've made, and you feel unable to forgive yourself for that failure; perhaps you even find yourself angry with God.

Whatever your trial right now, it seems that trying to straighten out the mess that's been made of your life seems as easy as trying to unscramble an egg. It seems absolutely *impossible* to ever undo the damage that has been done to your life. And so you ask God, "How can You let this happen to me? God, it's not fair!"

You're right—it isn't fair. But life itself often isn't fair. We live in a world in which evil often appears to be rewarded, and the innocent are made to suffer: "The race is not to the swift or the battle to the strong, nor does food come to the wise or wealth to the brilliant or favor to the learned; but time and chance happen to them all."[93] We don't live in a *fair* world; we live in an *unforgiving* world—a world of hostility, sin, and injustice.

What God wants you and me to know is that we *can* be whole people, even in an unforgiving world. We *can* be forgiving people, even in an unforgiving world. We *can* be people of unconditional love and Christlike character, even in an unforgiving world. We can be, and we *must* be, for that is the style of life that God has called us to.

You can find healing even in the face of all the harm and injustice that has been done to you. Though you feel you are nothing but a *victim*, you can be a *victor* through Jesus Christ. No, there are no "Ten Easy Steps to Victorious Christian Living," for there are no "easy" steps to developing Christlike maturity and proven character. But you can begin living your life in such a way that God will be able to use *any* circumstance in your life—even the *unfair* circumstances—to bring about growth, maturity, and proven Christlike character in your life.

We need to understand that God's will is not that we should have a life of ease and "smooth sailing." Rather, He wants us to know that His will for us is that we "be conformed to the likeness"—the image, the character—"of His Son."[94] How we need to grasp this central truth of the Christian life!

And how do we become conformed to the image of Christ? I'm convinced that this *only* happens through a process—an often difficult and painful process of refining each believer's character through the hard places of life. God can use those hard places in your life to *refine* and *define* your character for His glory—if you are open to what He wants to teach you.

Learning to Grow

Our goal is to become whole, forgiven followers of Christ, able to boldly stand and confront the injustice and sin of the world around us with the power of unconditional love. Our objective in life is *definition of character*—building into our lives the kind of mature character that is defined by the qualities that marked the life of Jesus. Let me share with you a few ways to start that healing, character-defining process in your life.

1. *Stop trying to justify yourself, even when you know you are right.* Do you want to be right, or do you want to be whole? You can't always be both. Sometimes, in order to be well and whole, you have to give up the luxury of being right. I know this is not easy advice to take. It is our nature as human beings to want to defend ourselves from attack, to justify ourselves, to counter-attack.

Please don't.

If your focus is on being *right*, you'll become mired in self-pity whenever you are misunderstood, opposed, or lied about. You'll become obsessed with defending yourself. In time that obsession will overcome every other consideration in your life, ruining your sleep, sapping your enjoyment of life, souring your outlook on life, damaging your relationships with God and other people, and destroying your spiritual, emotional, and even physical health.

Some of us feel we have to be right even when we know we're wrong. But if we're to become whole, we need to be able to say "I was wrong" without equivocation, without face-saving, without ifs, ands, or buts. In his profoundly helpful book about emotional, spiritual, and physical wholeness called *There's a Lot More to Health Than Not Being Sick,* Bruce Larson writes:

> When we are free to admit our errors, relationships have a new dimension. Most of us get into trouble because we judge other people by their actions and ourselves by our intentions, and, of course, *our* intentions are always good. When my wife is hurt or angry because of something I have done, I am immediately on the defensive. I remind her how much I love her and insist I'd never do anything to hurt her. I have a hard time believing I could have done anything unloving when my intentions were so good. How much all of my relationships would improve if I could attribute good intentions to those who hurt me and at the same time hold myself accountable for my actions, no matter how noble my intentions.
>
> I think we would have a positive hold on health and wholeness if we could live our lives by this royal rule. Make excuses for others—they meant well—but not for ourselves.[95]

If our focus is on being *well and whole*, then we no longer have to make excuses for ourselves, we no longer have to vindicate ourselves. We can let God be our defender, our vindication. We can rest in the knowledge that our defense is in the hands of Someone far more capable than we ourselves.

If our focus is on being *well and whole*, then we are free to attribute the best of motives even to the worst actions of other people. We become invulnerable to the attacks, slights, and indignities of others, and begin to live life as Christ lived—the life of a bold, courageous agent of love and forgiveness, able to act instead of always reacting, able to lovingly speak the truth without fearing the attacks and insults of others, able to demonstrate unconditional love and forgiveness even though surrounded by hostility and anger.

When you know in your heart that you have been *justified by faith* through the cross of Jesus Christ, when you are secure in the fact that you are justified in the eyes of God, then you don't need to be justified in the opinion of the public or any individual. You are liberated from the burden of having to be right; you can live free, whole, and forgiven.

2. *Don't try to convince the unconvinceable.* In Luke 9 Jesus sent out the disciples, telling them that if anyone would not receive their gospel, they were to shake the dust off their feet and move on. In other words, they were not to waste their time trying to convince the unconvinceable.

If your reputation has been smeared by gossip, or if someone opposes you out of a seemingly determined desire to misunderstand you, then it's pointless to try to convince the unconvinceable.

There will always be some people who seek to hear both sides, who will treat you fairly, who will refuse to judge you without giving you a chance to be heard. But there will also be many others who make a career out of thinking the worst, of passing quick judgment. With such people, what do you expect to accomplish by continuing to defend and justify yourself? Their minds won't change. Rather, they're likely to say, "Aha! On top of everything else that's wrong with you, you're *defensive*, too!"

You should unconditionally love the unconvinceable. Don't hold grudges or deliberately cut yourself off from them. But if you plainly can't win them over, then don't trouble yourself about them! Share yourself and your dreams with those people who affirm and encourage you and who share your vision.

3. *Understand that when you patiently withstand the misunderstanding, slander and unforgiveness of others, you find favor with God.* First Peter 2:20,21 tells us, "How is it to your credit if you receive a beating for doing wrong and endure it? But if you suffer for doing good and you endure it, this is commendable before God.

To this you were called, because Christ suffered for you, leaving you an example, that you should follow in His steps."

If you are trying to live a Christlike, Spirit-led life, then there is one thing you can count on: There will be times when you will be *rejected*. You will be *misunderstood*. You will be *lied about*. You will be *ridiculed*. When persecution comes, don't protest that it's unfair; don't think it's unnatural; don't lose heart. It comes with the territory, it comes with the committed Christian life, and it means *favor and blessing* for your life from God.

Blessing?

That's right. "*Blessed* are you when people insult you, persecute you and falsely say all kinds of evil against you because of me," said our Lord Jesus. "Rejoice and be glad, because great is your reward in heaven, for in the same way they persecuted the prophets who were before you."[96] The prophets were lied about, rejected, misunderstood, and killed. Jesus Himself was slandered, vilified, betrayed, and crucified. If you are a follower of Christ, you need to be aware that rejection and misunderstanding are part of your *heritage!*

One of the hardest things we will ever be called to do as Christians is to endure such a trial of being slandered or rejected. In fact, there is probably only one thing worse: watching someone close to you—a parent, a friend, or especially a husband or wife—endure such a trial. I've seen it happen over and over, as children have tearfully watched their parents denounce each other in the course of a bitter, scandalous divorce; as men and women have seen their working spouses victimized by rumor in the cruel game of office politics; as the wives of pastors have had to watch helplessly while their husbands were raked over the hot coals of a divided church. It's almost always harder on the one who stands by, watching it happen, than to the one who is the actual victim.

Often the one who endures such a trial will attempt to bear his burden with Christian grace, forgiveness, and obedience—and this will drive the victim's spouse crazy! "How can you just take it lying down? Why don't you defend yourself?" If that is your response to your loved one's trial, then you're not helping him; you're compounding the burden and stress of that trial, and making it that much harder for your loved one to undergo the trial with mature, Christlike strength of character.

If I've described your situation, then I urge you to begin supporting your loved one as he endeavors to meet adversity and opposition with Christlike forgiveness and unconditional love. Go to your knees in prayer for strength and wisdom for your loved one and for yourself. Pray that Jesus Christ will be seen and glorified in the courageous, obedient, persevering spirit that you and your loved one are displaying.

Character Defined

The apostle Paul knew what it meant to be persecuted, abused, misunderstood, and wounded by acts of unforgiveness. Throughout the book of Acts we witness Paul being lied about, misunderstood, opposed, beaten, tortured, stoned, and imprisoned—all for the "crime" of preaching the forgiving love of Jesus Christ. How did Paul respond to the trials that buffeted him throughout his Christian life? "When we are cursed, we bless; when we are persecuted, we endure it; when we are slandered, we answer kindly."[97] And then he gives this word of admonition: "I urge you to imitate me."[98] Why? Because Paul was *imitating Christ*, who also had been slandered, rejected, misunderstood, and ultimately even crucified—and yet never once opened His mouth in His own defense.

What was the response of our Lord when He was defamed and falsely accused and executed for a crime He never committed? "Father, forgive them, for they do not know what they are doing."

What was the response of Stephen as he was being stoned to death by the temple rulers while a hardened Pharisee named Saul stood by and gave approval? "Lord, do not hold this sin against them."[99]

I believe that it was in answer to this prayer of Stephen's—a prayer of forgiveness toward Saul and the others who were killing him—that God later reached down and took Saul by storm and transformed his hard Pharisaic heart into the loving, forgiving, dedicated heart of an apostle, the apostle Paul. And the world was *changed*—not just by the life of Paul, but by the forgiving prayer of Stephen.

I'm sure Paul had many occasions to remember the Christlike, forgiving example of Stephen, who was breathing out forgiveness as the last crushing stones were being hurled onto his bleeding, broken body. I'm sure Paul thought often of Stephen's faith and boldly defined character when he himself was undergoing slander and curses and beatings and stonings. And Paul's response to these trials was to bless, to endure, to answer kindly, to forgive.

The natural response to a situation in which we are rejected and defamed is to fight back. But God calls us, through the words and examples of His Son Jesus and such servants as Stephen and Paul, to a *supernatural* response—to forgiveness and unconditional love and courageous endurance. And there is only one way that such naturally frail, weak human beings as we can behave in powerful, superhuman, supernatural ways: by *relying on God*.

Don't rely on yourself. Don't rely on others. *Rely on God.* Reliance upon God is the only key to stability in the mountains and valleys of life. If you don't rely on God in times of elation, when everything is going great, then you will get too high; you will become proud and self-sufficient. If you don't rely on God in times of rejection, when your character is being defamed, when you are facing enormous opposition, then you will fall too low; you will lose your perspective and your Christian joy.

When others hurt you, oppose you, misunderstand you, then you need to pray continually for the strength to endure, to forgive, to love. You need to meditate continually in God's Word, looking especially to those passages which give you encouragement to forgive and to go on in times of opposition. You need to give blessing when you are cursed, and kind answers when you are slandered.

As Peter wrote to those who suffered persecution in the early church, "Rejoice that you participate in the sufferings of Christ, so that you may be overjoyed when His glory is revealed. If you are insulted because of the name of Christ, you are blessed, for the Spirit of glory and of God rests on you. . . . Those who suffer according to God's will should commit themselves to their faithful Creator and continue to do good."[100]

That's *definition of character*. That's a description of a life that is defined and shaped and sculpted by unconditional love and forgiveness. That's a life that is finding wholeness and completeness, even though surrounded by a hostile, unforgiving world.

A Healed Self-Image

Ultimately, a life that is made whole through forgiveness is a life that has attained God's peace, God's blessing, and the confident self-assurance of a completed self-image, of healed self-esteem. Let me share with you my own struggle toward self-forgiveness and a healed self-image.

As I was growing up, I was a "textbook-case younger brother," always coming in second in the sibling rivalry between myself and my brother Paul. Paul was a senior in high school when I was just entering as a freshman. He was an outstanding football player, basketball player, student council member, and lifeguard at the swimming pool. Sure, I competed successfully as a cross-country runner and gained recognition on the debate team, but somehow my achievements never had the luster of, say, Paul's scoring 25 points a game on the basketball court.

Thirsting for a self-esteem and self-acceptance based on accomplishments and recognition, I was programming myself for success, achievement, and excellence. But I found that my successes and achievements were never excellent enough. Even worse, I was unable to forgive myself for my failures. My achievements were unworthy, and I considered myself unworthy.

My sense of inadequacy carried over into other areas of life, so that I became unable to consider myself a truly *forgiven* person of worth and value unless I could accomplish something great and notable. Even after I gave my life to Christ, I continued for years to live with an inner struggle between my desire to serve

God and my yearning for recognition and success. I couldn't see myself as accepted and forgiven in God's sight.

As a result of my lack of self-forgiveness and self-esteem, I experienced great inner turmoil. This, I'm convinced, is what eventually led to sleeplessness and several physical ailments, as well as problems in my relationships with other people.

The irony of it all is that while I had struggled so long and so hard to fulfill my own ego and find peace with myself, I had been living all along with a man whose *entire life* was a Christlike act of love and forgiveness and acceptance. That man was my father.

Dad was a simple, caring man of God who was never very concerned with impressing others—how well he dressed, the length of his hair, the correct social graces. He had no driving desire to receive praise or recognition or glory; he had no grand ambitions for achieving greatness. His one concern was that his life might be an act of love, and thus he attained the greatest achievement of all: He affirmed others, he built the lives of others, and he impacted lives for Jesus Christ.

The singing group which I led for several years, The Children of Hope, came to love my father in a special way. While we were on tour one year, these young people took a collection and bought my father a plaque to congratulate him on his impending retirement. It read, "To Reverend Davis, 'I have fought the good fight, I have finished the course, and I have kept the faith.' With gratitude for your life of love, The Children of Hope."

The sanctuary was filled the night The Children of Hope gave a concert in our church in that small Iowa community. That night they presented the plaque to my father, knowing he was scheduled to retire in six months. He received the plaque with his usual spirit of grace and humility before the many people whom he had loved for so many years, and who loved him.

The next evening my father suffered a severe heart attack, and about two weeks later he went to be with the Lord. The last tribute to this man whose memory I treasure so much was entirely fitting. He had fought the good fight of faith; his course was nearly finished; his faith and his love held firm.

Shortly before my father's death, a friend of his asked him to write a short biography of his life. He did so, and ended that short book with his favorite poem, "That I Might Find My Savior's Heart," by Ralph Spalding Cushman. That poem hangs on the wall of my office, and I've taken its message as the creed for my life:

> I do not ask that crowds may throng the temple
> That standing room be priced,
> I only ask that as I voice the message
> They may see Christ.
>
> I do not ask for churchly pomp or pageant or music
> Such as wealth alone can buy,
> I only ask that as I voice the message
> Christ may be nigh.
>
> I do not ask that men may sound my praises
> Or headlines spread my name abroad,
> I only pray that as I voice the message
> Hearts may find God.
>
> I do not ask for earthly place or laurel
> Or of this world's distinctions any part,
> I only ask when I have voiced the message
> That I may find my Savior's heart.

A longtime friend of our family, a man who had been a missionary for many years, spoke at my father's funeral. He commented that people had always loved my father and been attracted to his life. Young people especially loved him, "not because he was 'cool,' " he said, "but because he *cared*."

Hearing those words, I knew they were a true description of the kind of life my dad had lived, and they brought me face-to-face with the shallow kind of "recognition game" I had been playing—a game with no end, no winning, no forgiveness, no real satisfaction.

God has brought many experiences into my life that have helped to refine and define my character, to shape it more and more into conformity with the character of Jesus Christ. Some of those experiences have been very hard; some have been times of refreshment and joyful discovery. Whether the experience has been pleasant or painful, I've gained the most and grown the most when I've been open to God's teaching and have relied on His goodness and mercy.

As I continue to live out my Christian pilgrimage, I am discovering that every act of service and witness for Jesus Christ will ultimately be either a filling station for my own ego or a "still more excellent way" to live for God.[101]

There is probably no emotional problem more common to us all than the struggle for self-esteem. What we need to keep on learning is that true self-esteem and self-forgiveness can never be found in anything except the love of God. We're not forgiven and valued because we can do some great service for God or achieve praise before men. We have value and worth *only* because God loved us enough to send Jesus to die for us. "Nothing in my hand I bring," says the hymn; "simply to Thy cross I cling."

God loved us when we had *no* value, *no* worth. His unconditional love, focused on our sin-wracked lives, gave us worth and meaning and peace. Today this same God of forgiveness is alongside us, healing us, making us truly whole, enabling us to live out His unconditional love and forgiveness to a hurting, dying, unforgiving world.

Because Christ died for us, we are forgiven. This fact alone is the reason we can forgive ourselves. And this fact *requires* that we be kind and compassionate to one another, forgiving each other, just as God through Christ has forgiven us.

Notes

1. 1 Corinthians 13:4-8,13.
2. Matthew 5:44; Luke 6:27.
3. 1 Corinthians 13:5,8.
4. Romans 5:8.
5. Hosea 3:1.
6. 2 Corinthians 5:17.
7. Romans 8:29; Galatians 4:19.
8. Acts 3:19.
9. Acts 26:20.
10. Luis Palau, *Experiencing God's Forgiveness* (Portland: Multnomah Press, 1984), p. 17.
11. 2 Peter 1:5-10.
12. Psalm 103:12.
13. Hebrews 10:17.
14. Philippians 3:13,14.
15. Ephesians 2:8,9.
16. Ephesians 2:10.
17. Hebrews 9:14.
18. 1 John 2:1.
19. Galatians 1:10.
20. 2 Samuel 11:27.
21. 2 Samuel 12:9.
22. 2 Samuel 12:13.
23. 2 Samuel 12:13.
24. Psalm 51:1,2,7,9,10.
25. 1 Kings 14:8.
26. 1 Corinthians 15:9.

27. 1 Timothy 1:13; see also Acts 22:4; 26:11; Galatians 1:13.
28. 1 Timothy 1:15,16.
29. John Claypool, *The Light Within You* (Waco: Word Books, 1983), p. 187.
30. Ibid., pp. 191-92.
31. Psalm 86:5; see also Isaiah 55:6,7; Hebrews 10:17; 1 John 1:9.
32. T. S. Eliot, *The Cocktail Party: A Comedy* (New York: Harcourt, Brace & Co., 1950), pp. 134-37.
33. 1 John 4:18.
34. Bruce Narramore and Bill Counts, *Guilt and Freedom* (Santa Ana: Vision House, 1974), p. 69.
35. Jerry Cook, *Love, Acceptance and Forgiveness* (Glendale: Regal Books, 1979).
36. 1 John 4:7.
37. Romans 15:7.
38. Colossians 3:13.
39. Cook, *Love. . . Forgiveness*, p. 16.
40. Acts 11:23,24.
41. 1 Thessalonians 5:11.
42. Tony Campolo, *It's Friday, But Sunday's Comin'* (Waco: Word, 1984).
43. Ephesians 3:10,11.
44. Ephesians 3:21.
45. Ephesians 5:25,26.
46. David Augsburger, *The Freedom of Forgiveness* (Chicago: Moody Press, 1970), pp. 96-97.
47. Philippians 1:15-18.
48. Romans 15:7.
49. 1 Corinthians 9:22.
50. 2 Timothy 2:23-25.
51. Leilani Watt, *Caught in the Conflict* (Eugene: Harvest House, 1984), pp. 30-31.
52. Acts 13:13.
53. 2 Timothy 4:11.
54. Romans 15:1,7.

55. Colossians 3:13.

56. Galatians 5:13-15.

57. Matthew 5:9.

58. Matthew 18:15.

59. Galatians 5:22,23;6:1.

60. James 5:16.

61. Matthew 5:23,24.

62. Colossians 3:13,14.

63. John 17:20-26.

64. Acts 1:8.

65. Galatians 5:20; Ephesians 4:31; Colossians 3:8.

66. Ephesians 4:31; Colossians 3:8.

67. Ephesians 4:31.

68. Ephesians 4:31.

69. Colossians 3:8.

70. Galatians 5:20,26; Philippians 2:3.

71. Romans 16:17,18; Galatians 5:20.

72. Galatians 5:20.

73. Ephesians 4:31.

74. Acts 26:14.

75. Ross Campbell, *How to Really Love Your Child* (Wheaton: Victor Books, 1977), p. 84.

76. Carol Tavris, *Anger: The Misunderstood Emotion* (New York: Simon & Schuster, 1982), pp. 123,129.

77. Ibid., pp. 128-29.

78. See also Exodus 34:6; Numbers 14:18; Psalm 86:15; 103:8; 145:8,9; Joel 2:13; Jonah 4:2.

79. James 1:19,20.

80. Proverbs 15:1.

81. Ecclesiastes 7:9; see also Genesis 49:5-7; Psalm 37:8; Proverbs 14:17; 16:32; 19:11,19; 22:24; 27:4; 29:8; 30:33.

82. Matthew 5:21-24; 2 Corinthians 12:20; Galatians 5:20; Colossians 3:8; 1 Timothy 2:8; James 1:19,20.

83. Matthew 5:21-24.

84. Matthew 5:23,24.

85. John 8:32.

86. Exodus 20:16.

87. 2 Corinthians 12:20.

88. Ephesians 4:31; see also Exodus 23:1; Leviticus 19:16; Proverbs 16:28; 17:9; Romans 1:29-32; 1 Corinthians 5:11; Ephesians 4:25,29; Colossians 3:8,9; James 3:3-12.

89. 1 Corinthians 8:1.

90. 2 Corinthians 2:10,11.

91. Matthew 18:15,16.

92. Ephesians 4:29.

93. Ecclesiastes 9:11.

94. Romans 8:29.

95. Bruce Larson, *There's a Lot More to Health Than Not Being Sick* (Waco: Word Books, 1981), p. 37.

96. Matthew 5:11,12.

97. 1 Corinthians 4:12,13.

98. 1 Corinthians 4:16.

99. Acts 7:60.

100. 1 Peter 4:13,14,19.

101. 1 Corinthians 12:31—13:13.

CHRISTIAN HERALD ASSOCIATION AND ITS MINISTRIES

CHRISTIAN HERALD ASSOCIATION, founded in 1878, publishes The Christian Herald Magazine, one of the leading interdenominational religious monthlies in America. Through its wide circulation, it brings inspiring articles and the latest news of religious developments to many families. From the magazine's pages came the initiative for CHRISTIAN HERALD CHILDREN and THE BOWERY MISSION, two individually supported not-for-profit corporations.

CHRISTIAN HERALD CHILDREN, established in 1894, is the name for a unique and dynamic ministry to disadvantaged children, offering hope and opportunities which would not otherwise be available for reasons of poverty and neglect. The goal is to develop each child's potential and to demonstrate Christian compassion and understanding to children in need.

Mont Lawn is a permanent camp located in Bushkill, Pennsylvania. It is the focal point of a ministry which provides a healthful "vacation with a purpose" to children who without it would be confined to the streets of the city. Up to 1000 children between the age of 7 and 11 come to Mont Lawn each year.

Christian Herald Children maintains year-round contact with children by means of a *City Youth Ministry.* Central to its philosophy is the belief that only through sustained relationships and demonstrated concern can individual lives be truly enriched. Special emphasis is on individual guidance, spiritual and family counseling and tutoring. This follow-up ministry to inner-city children culminates for many in financial assistance toward higher education and career counseling.

THE BOWERY MISSION, located at 227 Bowery, New York City, has since 1879 been reaching out to the lost men on the Bowery, offering them what could be their last chance to rebuild their lives. Every man is fed, clothed and ministered to. Countless numbers have entered the 90-day residential rehabilitation program at the Bowery Mission. A concentrated ministry of counseling, medical care, nutrition therapy, Bible study and Gospel services awakens a man to spiritual renewal within himself.

These ministries are supported solely by the voluntary contributions of individuals and by legacies and bequests. Contributions are tax deductible. Checks should be made out either to CHRISTIAN HERALD CHILDREN or to THE BOWERY MISSION.

Administrative Office: 40 Overlook Drive, Chappaqua, New York 10514
Telephone: (914) 769-9000